THE MAKINGS OF A LITTLE LEAGUE UMPIRE

MIKE PERRINE

iUniverse, Inc.
New York   Bloomington

THE MAKINGS OF A LITTLE LEAGUE UMPIRE

iUniverse books may be ordered through booksellers or by contacting:

iUniverse
1663 Liberty Drive
Bloomington, IN 47403
www.iuniverse.com
1-800-Authors (1-800-288-4677)

Because of the dynamic nature of the Internet, any Web addresses or links contained in this
book may have changed since publication and may no longer be valid. The views expressed
in this work are solely those of the author and do not necessarily reflect the views of the
publisher, and the publisher hereby disclaims any responsibility for them.

ISBN: 978-1-4401-9622-5 (pbk)
ISBN: 978-1-4401-9619-5 (cloth)
ISBN: 978-1-4401-9621-8 (ebook)

Printed in the United States of America

iUniverse rev. date: 12/30/09

My love and thanks to my wife, Barb, who spent too many hours proof-reading and making copies of the manuscript.

THE MAKING OF A LITTLE LEAGUE UMPIRE

1 FLINCHING AND BAD UMPIRING

I guess I was bitten around two years ago. I was in Albany, Georgia visiting my son, Stephen, his beautiful, Southern-belle wife, Suzanne, and their two children Michael and Sarah. Michael was enrolled in two Little League programs, the local Dixie League and the hand-picked players of the Travel League. I watched games of both leagues and really couldn't tell a lot of difference but Stephen and Michael were both very proud of the fact that Michael had been chosen amongst only about fifteen Albany players to play in the Travel League.

In one of Michael's games there was a plate and one base umpire. The plate umpire, a big black guy, flinched as a forty mile an hour fastball was foul-tipped and buzzed his ear. I didn't know if he was good or bad but I knew he was terrible. Flinching is an umpiring no-no. *Trust your equipment. If you're in the right stance, you're not gonna get hurt…if you don't flinch.* Yeah, right.

Flinching causes tipped balls to land in one's ears. Not a good thing and particularly stinging when coming off a bat faster than the initial pitch.

And I know all about flinching. Before Stephen got into Little League, I did some umpiring. With no training and no experience every game was an ordeal. One day I stupidly tried to do a game behind the plate when, for some reason, I did not have

1

a chest protector or mask. I probably flinched on every pinch and after a shot to an ear and another below an eye socket I moved behind the mound.

The black guy continued to flinch but I don't remember any ear strikes. The base umpire was a white guy and friends with Michael's other grandfather, Mike.

Michael's name is Stephen Michael Jr. but they call him Michael. I'm Michael Wilson, and Stephen is Stephen Michael Sr. And Mike is Mike. So there are two *Mikes,* a *Michael,* and a couple of Stephens. Only Mike and I are confused; the others seem to handle the jumble of similar names, everyone answering when they're supposed to…except Mike and me.

Anyway, the base umpire has no clue and makes one bad call after another. I don't remember the outcome only that I thought the umpiring was shameful. I returned to my home in Fort Myers and called the Lee County Recreational Department and told them I wanted to umpire Little League.

II. SPEED (OR LACK THEREOF)

My father ran the high hurdles for the University of Florida in the late 1920s. Any semblance of family speed died when he did in the early nineties. There's a family picture of him, forward leg straight out and well past the top rung of the hurdle, back leg bent at the knee and just getting ready to clear the rung, one arm bent in front of his chest, the other behind him ready to propel him onward, and eyes straight ahead; the classic form of the athletic hurdlers of yesteryear.

He also played football and captained the basketball team his senior year. At six feet two, he was a very tall college player and when the ball was re-jumped at center court after every point, the Gators had a big advantage.

As I entered my teens, I began to question his alleged college athleticism. He never took much interest in the athletics of his three sons and I always thought (and still do) that had he possessed the skills of a true athlete, he would have wanted to pass those skills to his boys. But he did not. Counting the eight years of high school athletics of George Jr., Ken, and me, George Sr. attended a total of four of our events.

I'm not sure if one can be taught *speed*. Speed *mechanics* perhaps, but George Sr. had nothing to say about my lack of speed.

After college my father actually played professional basketball. A win was worth $5, a loss only $2. It was twenty years before the NBA and professional leagues were mostly relegated to individual states.

During the depression he refereed basketball, and maybe being a game official was the genetic handoff because he certainly didn't give me any of his athleticism or speed.

Michael suffers from a two generation affliction of speed deprivation and while he has good form and *looks* fast, he isn't. He seems to have twenty-four inch legs and a foot size to match.

Two generations of slug-like speed give him little chance at world records. He is too far removed from the hurdle speed of his paternal grandfather. And his maternal grandfather's genes have supplemented his plight.

Michael is a good kid and lives baseball. Like his father Stephen, Michael loves all sports. He plays middle school football, basketball, and Little League baseball. He's a good hitter and Stephen has purchased him series of pitching lessons from the local college baseball coach. He has an excellent pitching motion and an outstanding batting stroke. He turns into a pitch and finishes the swing with his back hand leaving the bat handle like the Major Leaguers, the bat and left hand turned all the way around his clearing hips. Michael hits with power. He's hit a number of triples and doubles the last couple of years. I don't know if he's ever cleared a fence but he's hit a lot of balls *to* the fence.

He's a catcher sometimes, and like his father, an outstanding defensive catcher. Michael has a decent arm unlike his father, and like his father, he's slow.

So there you have it…three generations of non-speed. Everyone would have been decent athletes had we been gifted with even a semblance of speed. I'm wondering too if each generation isn't getting slower. Maybe in the far future, one of us won't be able to move, our speed genes genetically eroded to mush.

I watched Michael drill a shot to left-center. Both fielders gave chase and at the *ping!* of the aluminum bat, I'm thinking "Certainly double, maybe triple!" But as Michael made the turn at first the ball had been chased down and the center fielder was cocking his arm.

From his third base coaching box Stephen yelled, "Back! Back!" and Michael retreated, embarrassed. Hey, accept it kid.

I keep telling his father, "He'll get bigger, stronger, meaner." But he's not going to make the U.S. Olympic track team.

Being a sprinter isn't critical in umpiring but you do have to hustle down the base paths and into the outfield to make calls. And a lot of Little League ball is done only with the plate umpire, a situation that demands a lot of field coverage by one person.

III. THE EARLY YEARS

When I was a kid, we played catch all day, EVERY day. We learned to throw and catch at an early age. My father bought me a Ted Kluzewski first baseman's mitt when I was ten. It was beautiful genuine leather inscribed with Ted's signature. I soon had it oiled and supple. I think it cost about $25.00, a huge amount of money back then.

Earle Cortright was entrenched at first base on our Little League team. A childhood pal and we remained close for years.

The coach took a look at my new mitt and assumed correctly that I also wanted to play first. Earle, however, was an outstanding hitter. He and his younger brother Jeff were both great ball players; good hitters, good athletes, good arms. I couldn't hit my shadow but I could throw and catch, and I soon learned to play first base as well as any eight year old. I eventually won the job and Earle grudgingly moved to short.

Earle and I both also pitched. Earle could throw fire whereas my fastball floated. But for some reason, and without trying, I would occasionally throw a ball that would fall off a cliff at the plate. I remember Johnny Church the catcher saying, "Mike, I can't believe you can throw that. Sometimes your pitches dive all over the place. How do you do it?" I didn't know; I just threw the damn baseball and sometimes it would break

Fifteen years later I tried out for the University of Maryland baseball team as a pitcher and threw twenty minutes of batting practice.

I threw my first pitch and it came back at me so fast I ducked; it sounded like an angry hornet. My pitches were all over the place, in the dirt, inside, outside, over the batter's head. I *still* couldn't pitch and I became extremely worried about plunking a batter. These guys were huge and I had morbid thoughts about skulling a batter, the batter dropping his bat and charging the mound.

A ball would rocket towards me either airborne or spinning off the infield. I would dance out of the way or dive for the dirt.

It was like the Charlie Brown cartoon; the ball rockets past him and he's knocked in the air, upside down, feet apart, his glove, hat, shoes, and socks flying.

I still had my floater and a curve ball that now hung suspended and the Terrapin studs crushed them to smithereens.

IV. EARLY ENCOUNTERS

When I coached Stephen's Little League team thirty years ago I was thrown out of too many games. We weren't very talented and my coaching was rank amateurish at best. I cheated, prodded, and schemed for every win.

As a Little League player in the 1950s, I learned a hidden ball trick that I successfully pulled a couple of times. A batter would be issued a walk and I'd stroll towards the mound, triggering the "play". Usually the first base coach was just another kid picking his nose and no one else was very interested in another of a million Little League walks. Johnny, our catcher, would call time and also go to the mound, allegedly to console the pitcher. The rest of our infield would convene and Johnny would slip the ball into my big Ted Kluzewski first baseman's mitt. I'd pat the pitcher's butt with the closed mitt and go back to the bag, trying to get behind the peripheral vision of the runner. Our pitcher would deliberately stay off the rubber and play with an imaginary baseball deep in his glove's pocket, as if trying to achieve the perfect curveball grip. In Little League a runner can't do *anything* if the pitcher toes the rubber; he can't leave the base until a pitched ball reaches the batter; but if the pitcher is *not* on or straddling the rubber, he can do anything he wants. If the runner made *the* mistake, his ass belonged to me.

During one of Stephen's games I was using him as my first baseman. He had been behind the plate in our last three games and needed a break from catching. Donald Broadley was pitching and the game was lost each time I penciled him in as our starter. Donald's fast ball smoothed in at twenty five miles an hour and he got shelled every time he pitched. He claimed to have a curve ball but *that* pitch would float in the size of a beach ball and the hitters would tee off. Donald was a neat kid, very intelligent, a hard worker, and he *could* throw it over the plate.

He and Stephen were the best of friends and the two of them constantly worked on Donald's "curveball." The Broadleys lived five houses away from our cul-de-sac and Stephen and Donald would throw to each other in the street in front of our house.

Stephen had a bad, ingrained throwing motion that I simply could not correct: as a right-handed thrower, he would push off his left foot. Of course it killed any velocity. I'd watch the two of them playing catch, Donald gripping his "curveball" and Stephen pushing off the wrong foot and wonder what I was doing coaching baseball.

Donald issues a walk and the "play" is on. I hadn't bothered to teach the intricacies of the hidden ball trick but Stephen could nevertheless pull it off. Somehow, Stephen got the ball from the catcher and returned to first base, waiting. It was a two-man umpiring crew and if there's only the first base runner, the first base ump should *back* to the B position, watching for anything at first base before the pitcher is ready to deliver to the next batter. I mean it's the base umpire's *only* responsibility; there are no fair-foul issues going on, no catch-no catch demands; absolutely nothing to do but watch first base while backing up to the B slot near second base. But not this umpire.

The runner naturally steps off the bag and Stephen tags the kid so hard he almost knocks him down. *Nothing*. A no-call; the teenage umpire picking zits instead.

It's the third inning, we're getting killed, we're already close to the mercy rule, I'm in a bad mood, and rocket from our dugout.

"He stepped off the bag! He's out!" I bark, my nose next to his.

"I didn't see anything," he says, realizing he's missed the play.

"You weren't looking, gawdammit. Why aren't you paying attention?"

I knew my remaining game time was severely limited, didn't care, and turned to the plate umpire.

"Did you see him step off the bag?"

"It's not my call."

"I don't care whose call it is; did ... you ... see ... him ... step ... off ... the ... bag?" I asked again, sarcastically.

"I didn't see anything," he lies.

I go back to first and again confront the base umpire.

"You're a piece of crap," I shout, sealing my ejection. "Pick your pimples someplace other than a baseball game ... '*Umpire*'."

He tosses me and I return to our dugout, fire up a Marlboro and singe my nasal passages, smoke billowing like a jet exhaust.

V. BIG FOOT

I remember the first athletic event George Sr. ever attended in which one of his sons was participating, a track meet, Miami Edison Senior High against several other Miami high school teams. I was eleven and in the sixth grade; Ken fourteen in the ninth grade, and George Jr. a senior in high school. He was 6-2, as tall as his father, ran the mile, and had the feet of a Grebe. Long distance running was the dumping ground of the track team; *any* one could be a miler.

In all of Miami there did not exist size fifteen track shoes. It was 1952 and the track shoes resembled ballet slippers with sharp spikes in the front soles, supposedly to better tear through the cinders of the track, akin to the exploding turf of bounding thoroughbreds. This was true especially of the sprinters; they would dash down the track, leaving contrails of flying cinders and dust.

I always thought it would be cool to do that, to leave erupting footsteps behind me as I hurtled down my lane towards a world record in the 100-yard dash. It never happened. I sprinted slower than even my slow-footed oldest brother.

The track meet was to be a family outing and I remember the gaiety of anticipation as each of us mused at the hilarity of George actually racing against other runners. In today's vernacular he was a klutz, maybe the most non-athletic member of his five-hundred student senior class.

He had tried out for the Junior Varsity football team when he moved from Horace Mann Junior High to Miami Edison High School. After a few days of mid-summer try-outs, the coaches suggested he would better serve the Red Raiders as a team manager. I remember being embarrassed at his title; he was no more than a water boy.

But in my mind, things would level out, the cream would rise to the top, the youngest son would make the family proud, making high-school All-American in football, basketball, and maybe even baseball.

George Jr. took his place beside the other milers and like the others, began jiggling his arms and legs, pumping his knees, closing his eyes, and doing a silly dance. I think he was just copying the other kids; this was his first competition and we all were *sure* he didn't have a clue about what he was doing. He put a Keds tennis shoe into each starting block and kicked backward, alternating each foot as runners do while priming for the start. Ten runners, everyone crouched and ready, nine of them with spiked track shoes and George in a pair of high-topped black Keds. A large black star within a white circle was pasted to the inside ankle of each shoe. The size fifteens stood out like snow shoes. The only redeeming thing about George Jr.'s appearance that night was the Keds' white laces.

The starter's pistol went off and the ten high school milers exploded off the start, George the last kid out of the blocks. The giggles rippled through the family as George settled into tenth place, the black clown shoes flopping along the cinders.

Going into the last lap of the four-lap mile race, George was still last but surprisingly, he had not lost any ground since the beginning of the second lap.

What happened next has stayed with me for the almost sixty years since that track meet. I will never forget it. George began overtaking runners and passed the last one with four hundred yards to the finish line. The four of us were stunned. The Edison fans erupted into "C'mon, George, C'mon!" It was delirium. A tall, lanky, stumblebum of a kid, wearing Keds tennis shoes outrunning the best high school milers in Miami. People in the stands were on their feet, screaming. Even non-Edison fans picked up on the improbability of what was happening and there seemed not a soul who was not on his feet, begging George to "C'mon, C'mon!!"

But another miler from Jackson High had George in his sights. He was 5-10, skinny as a rail with a long, graceful, effortless stride that started gobbling up the track between them. *This* was a miler. With George now only ten or fifteen yards ahead, the kid downshifted, floored his racing accelerator, and flew past a gasping George, winning easily. But my brother hung on for second and the family gaiety turned to wondrous pride.

I'll never forget my father's "compliment". "You almost had it. Maybe we can find you some track shoes if you're going to keep running."

VI. THE REAL ATHLETES

When Ken got to high school, he loved basketball and towered over the other players on the Junior Varsity team. The summer before high school, Ken grew over eight inches. You could *watch* him grow. But he was not a starter and in a home game that George Sr. attended, the coach inserted him in the third quarter. Ken took a shot that circled the rim, slowed, stopped, teetered, and dropped through the net. As Ken's first two points of the season registered on the gym's electronic scoreboard he gave out a *"YAHOOOOO!"* and ran to his defensive post with a huge grin. Then he made one of two free throws. Later he made another basket and with five points in about seven minutes, Ken was feeling good about his game and himself. Towards the end, Ken was benched with no more points but still felt he had contributed to the team's losing effort.

Later my father's only comment was, "You need to hustle more; hustle will overcome lack of skill." Ken was crushed. His father's biting words have stayed with him for over fifty years.

Every skirt in Miami Edison Senior High had an eye on the big, handsome guy when his sophomore year started. But Ken was picky; all through high school he dated only the pristine beauties, gorgeous young ladies who went on to college and married into riches and politics. Ken's girlfriends were the upper crust of

Miami Shores, the blueblood neighborhood that partially fed the Edison student body. *All* of his girlfriends were tall brunettes; true teenage beauties, girls that, during my pre-puberty years, created an inner urgency to get older and to get there quickly.

I've been a couple of thousand votes away from a White House dinner invitation. A tall, gorgeous brunette fell in love with Ken, and our whole family was taken by her beauty, brains, beautiful smile, and personality. She was voted *Most Beautiful* in her senior year, made straight As, and loved my brother like no other. For reasons that still dumbfound the remaining family, Ken broke up with her and she married a very rich man who became the governor, a U.S. Senator, and later a candidate for the President of the United States.

Ken ran the one hundred yard dash ("meters" had not yet been invented) in eleven flat and high jumped over six feet. And he was brainy. His IQ hovers around one seventy but he was the reincarnation of the 1920s *Gentlemen Make Cs*. Somehow with his mediocre high school grades he followed George Jr. into Duke University despite very tough admission standards. In those days nepotism was part of Duke's admission strategies and George Jr. had done well at the Durham, North Carolina campus. His excellent grades and a pre-med undergraduate curriculum were Ken's admission ticket.

Ken continued his Cs at Duke but his finances quickly evaporated because his father had squandered all of his available money on George Jr.'s education, including a brand new 1956 Ford Fairlane. That left the rest of us monetarily screwed so Ken dropped out of Duke and joined the Navy. He became an Aviation Electronics Technician and after several months of Navy electronic schools, received orders to the U.S.S. Randolph, a WWII aircraft carrier. He was assigned to the helicopter squadron that plucked Alan Shepard from the Atlantic after the world's first manned sub-orbital space flight.

After four years Ken had developed a genuine dislike for that part of the Navy officer corps made up of Annapolis graduates.

And most of his squadron officers were Academy ensigns so he took his four year honorable discharge and reentered Duke. He got his B.S., a Masters, and a PhD all on his Navy savings and by flipping hamburgers forty hours a week for five years. And he didn't ask his father for a plug nickel.

To this day Ken and I still harbor resentment for the blatant favoritism. George Jr. had everything paid for, everything; even his four years of medical school and his two-year internship. Our father shelled out money for George Jr.'s M.D. as if his retirement depended on it. But when he died in a V.A. hospital fifteen years after his oldest son had begun a private practice in Ohio, George Sr. had not been repaid a penny. In fact, Ken nursed him through his terminal months, driving back and forth from Aiken, South Carolina to central Florida dozens of times to comfort his dying father.

Ken's son, Danny, is in his mid thirties, very tall, and should have played on the PGA tour. Occasionally he can still shoot in the high sixties.

A few years back Stephen, Danny, and I were playing Danny's home course, Hounds Lake, in Aiken, South Carolina. It was a grand day, a father/uncle playing golf with his son and nephew. Stephen is six-two, Danny six-five. At the turn we went into the clubhouse for a beer and I still remember everyone turning to look at the two tall, handsome young men. They're both good-looking, intelligent, and gifted young adults and I'm very proud of both of them.

The kids were hitting from the blues, me from the whites. They're on the elevated tee of number sixteen, a 590 yard par-5, dogleg left. There's a lake in front of the elevated green, a 180-yard carry. The fairway is sloped towards the lake so a good tee shot will roll forever.

What I remember most about Danny's tee shot were the gasps Stephen and I uttered as the Titleist left his driver. The ball soared majestically and obediently turned left at the dogleg. It hit and bounded towards the lake. To this day it is the longest golf shot I've ever witnessed. Danny hit an eight iron to the pin. I'm still hitting driver at 180 yards!

I also remember Danny missing the ten-foot eagle and flinging his putter at the golf cart as we walked off the green, knocking off a hubcap while Stephen and I roared.

VII. J.V. HEROICS

My father saw two of my high school athletic events.

I too made the junior varsity basketball team when I reached tenth grade. I was short and slow and had a jump shot that I would throw up after elevating three or four inches.

With the varsity hogging the indoor gym at every practice, the junior varsity was relegated to the asphalt courts on the roof of the gym. The Miami heat radiated off the surface, cooking us.

The scrimmages were enjoyable but the practice-ending wind sprints sadistic. We'd line up at the side of one of the two courts and race across both courts, slam into the chain link fence, turn, and race back. Immediately after I finished the coach's whistle would blow and we'd regroup at the start and run again, and again, and again. I guess we had twelve players and I don't think I ever won a wind sprint.

It was in the days before coaches knew of the existence of water. Water was for sissies, non-athletes, guys who couldn't cut it. If today's jocks were treated like we were, a lot of people would be dead and a lot of coaches in jail.

George Sr. watched only one of my basketball games, a home game against the Coral Gables High Junior Varsity. Our coach promised that everyone would play a half. My "half" was disastrous. I immediately fouled a kid who was driving against me and he made both of the one-and-one shots. Moments later a Gables kid stole my dribble and put in an uncontested layup. The next time I had the ball I dribbled it off the side of one of my Chuck Taylors, out of bounds. A pass was intercepted and within minutes I had led a ten-point Coral Gables swing. All of the ten point turnaround was my personal donation but I still couldn't believe it when a teammate tapped me on the shoulder. "I need a little more time to warm up," I thought, livid that the coach had lied. After the game George Sr. said nothing, his disgust overwhelming his ability to speak

VIII. TOM AND THE GUNGA-DIN

Tom Calhoun and I became friends in the seventh grade; we're now pushing seventy. We lost contact for over fifty years and I've missed him like a brother.

In high school we became skilled skirt-chasers, advanced beer drinkers, and magnets for trouble.

We played two partial years of high school football but we didn't have any business on a high school team. But as juniors we were members of an undefeated team and we milked it. I don't think any skirt at Edison could have identified us as the football slackers we were, especially the sophomore coeds. *Their* football heroes were still the JV kids so any stud on the varsity was therefore idolized. To Tom and me that meant every weekend night presented opportunities for trouble making and for back seat

conquests.

Tom and I had played junior varsity football but not well and quit the team half way through the season. We had become the best of friends and had gone through the sophomore schedule for five games, played very little, and soon tired of the endless practices and wind sprints. There were better things to do than get beat up every day.

A year later, as juniors, and after the varsity won its first game of the season against a good North Miami squad, Tom and I asked Jack Powers, the varsity coach, if we could join the team. We knew that because we had quit the JV team and then missed the punishing two-a-day summer workouts for the varsity, we didn't stand much of a chance. Only because Coach Powers was a friend of my father's did he allow us to suit up.

To have quit JV and then beg the varsity head coach to allow us on the team put us on the lowest rung of team chemistry, of team camaraderie. We were outsiders, unwelcome, not wanted, and in the way.

We were immediately assigned to the "Gunga Din" squad, about ten players who didn't have the skills, maturity, or speed to ever be called football players. The Gunga Dins were tackling and blocking dummies. We'd put on our jockstraps, shoulder pads, hip pads, knee pads, pants, jerseys, and helmets just like everyone else each day and then get our asses stomped. I'm sure there was an effort to run us off the team, both a coaching effort and a teammate effort.

I remember a kid named Jimmy Speed. Jimmy was 6-3, 220 pounds with rippling muscles, fast, and dumb as a stump. Jimmy punted for the Red Raiders that year and won a scholarship to a large southern university for his kicking skills. But I don't think he ever finished Edison; he was a moron.

One day, preparing for our last scheduled game against the hated Miami High Sting Rays, the coaches designed a two-on-one drill, another Gunga Din and me against Jimmy. They wanted us to emulate Miami's blocking half back, a very strong speedster who would explode out of his stance and annihilate anyone threatening his trailing runner. The kid would come at the defensive end or corner and throw himself at the defender. He was so good that the famous "Sting Ray Sweep" became "Sweep 36," his jersey number. Miami had lost only once coming into this game and a Sting Ray win was expected. "Sweep 36" was

Miami's bread and butter play. Everyone knew it was coming but no one had been able to stop it.

The Miami High-Edison High football rivalry was lopsided; we had beaten them only once since the series began in the 1920s. Every year it was the same; Edison would go into the game with a good record or even undefeated, and get thrashed. Our one win was around 1952 when Edison ran from the single wing formation, a football offensive system that was archaic even then. Somehow Edison won that game and our family watched George Jr. haul water buckets and towels on and off the field during time outs.

If we could stop "Sweep 36" we had a chance to win. Our regular defensive end had suffered a broken jaw in the last game and Jimmy was the replacement. The purpose of the drill was for Jimmy to turn the play, turn it inside so that a linebacker or cornerback could move up and make the hit on the runner. If Jimmy allowed the play to go outside, the Sting Rays would gobble up huge chunks of yardage. Play after play after play, we were thrown against Jimmy the Gorilla. The other Gunga Din and I would alternate roles, one of us playing the role of the Miami High blocking back, the other the ball carrier. An assistant coach stood nearby, yelling "Go!" as the drill was run again and again.

Early in the drill Jimmy would step into the path of the blocking back, drive him into the ground with a massive forearm, and take down the runner. Actually Jimmy's technique wasn't that good but with our lack of strength and speed, the two Gunga Dins were easy pickings. I didn't think Jimmy was getting low enough but remember being puzzled that the coach hadn't said anything.

The drill seemed to last forever and towards the end, Jimmy was as tired as we were. Jimmy and I would stand ten yards apart, our tongues hanging out, gasping for air that wasn't there, our shoulders heaving, peering at each other, and silently begging the other for respite. At "Go!" I would grudgingly come out of my stance and run at him. The initial impact was forearms to forearms. Jimmy had enormous upper body strength and I was in agony, my chest, shoulders, and forearms beaten to a pulp. The other Gunga Din was limping and blood oozed from a nostril.

The thought occurred to me to try and get lower on Jimmy and on the next play, I sauntered at him as usual but just before another of his punishing forearm jolts, I rolled into his knees. Jimmy was on his derriere and suddenly the Gunga Dins had turned the corner on bad-ass Jimmy Speed.

Hugh Farrell was the assistant coach conducting the drill. Coach Farrell had been an All-American defensive lineman at UNC, was built like a tank, and approached high school football practices like a marauding hyena. He loved violence, dirt, and blood, and often went one-on-one with his defensive linemen in punishing drills.

He ran at Speed, snatched fistfuls of jersey, put his nose against Jimmy's, and screamed unintelligible rants, his spittle hitting Jimmy's face. It was a time before facemasks and helmet cages. We only wore mouth pieces and Farrell was deliberately loading saliva. He extended his arms and began yanking Jimmy back and forth like a rag doll.

The entire practice field stopped other drills, turned and watched. Jimmy's head was snapping back and forth, his knees ready to buckle, his arms flopping, and his face covered with Coach Farrell's spit. The other Gunga Din and I watched in awe; the beast who minutes earlier had punished us unmercifully was now being pummeled by a man five inches shorter.

The drill resumed and Jimmy's knees became our blocking targets. We had taken all the punishment Jimmy could give and suddenly it seemed like we were on even terms. We practically had him on the ropes and despite Coach Farrell's anger, he was more worried about his knee cartilages than a Miami High touchdown. We were still getting beaten up but occasionally one of us would get a decent block on Jimmy while the runner got outside. On these plays Coach Farrell would merely stand there with a terrible scowl on his face, his neck veins bulging.

I wanted to exact at least a fraction of the punishment Jimmy had given me, and while targeting one's knees is considered football atrocity, I didn't care. After knocking Speed on his butt, my confidence was surging, my adrenalin pumping, and my stamina building with each "GO!" I was standing up to and sometimes defeating the biggest guy I had ever faced! For that one day, and the only day of my life, I was a real football player. I was dirty, bloody, tired, and sore, but I had knocked Jimmy Speed on his ass a number of times.

Despite my inner joy, no one said diddly squat to me about the drill except Coach Farrell.

"Now you know what it's like," he grinned as I limped past him on the way to wind sprints. I don't know if the drills helped but during the game and after a couple of Hugh Farrell death threats, Jimmy began to win the war against the speedy Miami High blocking back.

During pre-game warm-ups for the game, with both teams on the field, and the Orange Bowl crowd building to almost forty thousand, someone told Tom and me to go downfield about forty yards and retrieve Jimmy Speed's practice punts.

Jimmy rivaled the best punters in the NFL. The ball would explode off his right foot, spiral to the heavens, and stay suspended in mid-air forever.

I wasn't an athlete but I was athletic; that is, I could catch and throw and do a lot of athletic moves well. I would settle under Speed's punts, time their descent, and softly cradle the football as it came at me.

Tom, on the other hand, was as klutzy as George Jr. We were positioned in front of the Miami High student section, separated only by the sideline. Tom and I took turns catching Speed's booming punts. When it was Tom's turn, he would stagger around looking like a drunken sot trying to untangle his feet.

After a couple of Speed's punts had ricocheted off Tom the hilarity was obvious to both me and the Miami High student section. It was riotous. The razzing became giggles, the giggles explosive guffawing. The ball would come spinning down, hit Tom in the chest or a shoulder pad, rebound skyward, and *then* he would flail drunkenly at the ball. I had never seen a football do what those footballs were doing. My shoulders and belly were heaving with raucous laughter and I had to turn away from the students. I continued laughing throughout pre-game and into the game itself.

IX. TOM AND THE LETTERMEN

We beat the Miami Stingrays, won all of our ten scheduled games, the Miami city championship, and were invited to a postseason game which was also held in the Miami Orange Bowl. This was the other high school athletic event that my father attended.

We were playing a team from New Jersey and Tom and I had not played all year, not once, not even in the games the Red Raiders won by landslides. It was our punishment for the cheap way we had become team members. The coaches didn't like us, our fellow players had no respect for us, and our parents were embarrassed.

Back then everyone but the starters wore black high-tops, high-laced shoes with black laces and cleated soles that, given my lack of foot speed, felt like lead. The guys who played wore cool low-cuts and *looked* like football players.

I could run the one-hundred yard dash, barefoot, in fourteen seconds flat, Tom about fourteen five, so the end-of-practice wind sprints were tortuous. Perhaps fifty kids, everyone in full gear, and everyone out-sprinting me and Tom. High-tops, low-cuts, it didn't matter, we were *always* last.

But Tom and I played it to the hilt. Seven or eight games into the season, undefeated, me a Gunga-Din quarterback and outside linebacker; Tom a Gunga-Din corner.

Who gave a shit that we never played a down? Hammering some gal in the back seat of my '57 Chevy or Tom getting it on with his girlfriend in his parents' basement, and our splintered asses never got mentioned. We were members of the undefeated Red Raiders, we were Edison football players, and we were gridiron greats.

On the day of the postseason game Tom and I were hanging out in the student parking lot. Another student had left his '57 Pontiac station wagon unlocked. In the back, in full view, was a beautiful pair of black football low-cuts. I tried the latch, opened the rear gate, and snatched them. They were a perfect 10 ½ with white laces and another lace woven through loops around the ankles. It was the days of the Oklahoma Sooners, Paul Hornung, Tommy McDonald, and speedy halfbacks wearing low-cuts.

Before the game in our dressing room, before getting bused to the Orange Bowl, I slipped on the stolen low-cuts, wanting a full-length mirror to capture the image. An assistant coach walked by, looked at my shoes, frowned, and moved on.

In my mind I was starting because I *looked* like a football player, a guy who had suddenly gained several seconds in the one hundred yard dash, a starter, a damn star. What the hell if I never played a down?

As the game wound down, Edison was kicking butt, something like 45-7 and Coach Powers ambled down our sidelines, motioning guys into the game. *Any* game time was a football letter on your Edison sweater. He was getting everyone in, making sure everyone on the team got a letter. Everyone that is, except Tom and me. He stopped in front of Tom, looked at him, said nothing, and moved to me. He looked at me and continued. I don't know if I was relieved or disappointed. Everyone out there could outrun me, even the fat field judge, and I still have morbid thoughts of some New Jersey kid racing around my cemented low-cuts for a last-minute touchdown. So Tom and I did not letter in football, the only two guys on the team who didn't.

After the game George Sr. asked, "What number were you?"

"Sixty-nine," I lied, and was relieved that he did not ask me if I had gotten in.

X. BOMBS AWAY

It was a Saturday and Tom and I ambled into a Miami Beach high rise hotel, the Eden Roc. We were good at deception, the desk clerk giving us only a cursory look as we went straight to the elevators.

We had been here previously, on a Friday afternoon weeks before. On that day we had strolled into the lobby, looked at some brochures, and walked aimlessly outside to the large swimming pool adjacent to the Atlantic Ocean. We frolicked in the pool, flirted with two-piece swimsuits and ordered four cold beers using a fake room number. We scrawled a very nice tip on the ticket and scribbled an illegible signature. It was a very entertaining afternoon but on the serious side we *had* cased the lobby, information we could use later.

This Saturday night we entered the lobby and as we turned a corner to the elevators, I said to the desk clerk, "How ya' doin'?" We must have looked every bit like we knew where we were going, thanks to our earlier reconnaissance.

We aimlessly went to the 15th floor and walked the hallway searching for something to do. The Eden Roc was a north-to-south building, the front rooms overlooking a pretty inland waterway, Indian Creek, lying to the west, and the back rooms overlooking the Atlantic.

Huge yachts bobbed in Indian Creek, tied to the piers of the estates that lined the west bank of the small waterway. Shimmering lights from the yachts and the mansions danced on the calm waters. We were no more than two or three hundred yards from the ultra rich of Miami Beach.

It was around midnight and we didn't see any room doors ajar, nothing to do; no strolling women, nothing. As I was about to push the down elevator button I heard Tom say, "Noooo shit!" I walked to the end of the hall where he was standing and there, on an open balcony fifteen stories up, was a five hundred pound urn packed with dirt and a small palm tree. There was an urn and baby palm tree on both ends of every Eden Roc floor.

"C'mon." he ordered, putting a shoulder into the urn. The urn was sitting on a waist-high, twenty inch thick wall. Straight down was an east-to-west alley. I looked and saw nothing but a garbage bin. The bottom was mostly dark, street lights from Collins Avenue cast a muted glow into the west entrance. I put a shoulder into the urn along with Tom and gradually it began to inch towards the edge.

I remember our elation as it toppled over; elation that turned to horror when, after too long, it had not hit. We waited and waited, not understanding the delay. Suddenly, the urn, dirt, and baby palm tree exploded on the pavement and a low rumble crawled towards the opening of the alley onto Collins Avenue. Escaping the confines of the two hotels, the report turned apocalyptic. The shockwave climbed up the walls of the Eden Roc and the adjacent hotel, hit Tom and me, and knocked us back into the hall.

As a four year old I lost the hearing in my right ear because of measles-induced nerve damage and I was afraid the drum of my only remaining good ear would shatter when the painful blast reached us. We staggered, regained our balance, and sprinted for the elevator doors.

I remember thoughts of the two buildings collapsing, their bottom floors blown away. We had to escape the disintegrating

Eden Roc and we had to evade capture; cops and security people would be swarming all over, hunting us. We descended and Tom pushed the eighth floor button. We were sure there were people in the lobby watching the floor indicator lights, plotting our interception and capture; others racing up stairwells and still others riding up the adjacent elevator.

I don't remember how we got out of the Eden Roc that night, only that it wasn't a conventional exit; probably through an air conditioning duct. I do remember Tom and me dropping about ten feet to the pavement in the alley on the north side of the building. We ran to Tom's 1956 Ford, got in, and sat in the darkness, too afraid to move or talk.

No sirens, yet. A few minutes longer and we still had not heard anything. In another thirty minutes our fright turned to disappointment.

Our adrenalin fading, Tom cranked the Ford and we drove nonchalantly past the Eden Roc. There were no police cars, no ambulances, no people swarming, nothing. The alleyway was too dark to see the aftermath of our self-made nuclear detonation.

The explosion apparently excited no one on Miami Beach except Tom and me.

XI. FLYING SAUCERS AND DR. WALSH

The Eden Roc caper was insignificant compared to some of the escapades Tom and I pulled.

One Friday, Tom, Earle, and I spent the night together. Tom's parents were out of town and Earle and I took turns calling our parents to stay at the other's house. We got into Tom's parents' wine and spent a couple of hours telling jokes and stories and bragging about sexual conquests.

The original idea was Tom's. Around 2:00am he called the Daily News, Miami's evening newspaper. He used a fake voice and screamed, "This is Doctor Lou Walsh, I live in Miami Shores and there are little green people climbing down ladders onto my roof. There are flying saucers hovering above my house!" We continued the calls until 6:00am, changing our voices and the names to other Miami Shores residents. Because Tom had done the original Dr. Walsh, he called back at 3:00am.

He asked frantically, "Why haven't you done anything? Now they're in my kitchen and using my bathroom!" as Earle and I heaved with laughter.

To our astonishment, the Miami Daily News printed the story on the front page of the next night's edition. The first paragraphs started at the bottom right and continued on page four.

Ralph Rennick, a popular TV Channel 4 newscaster picked up the story and presented his version on the evening newscast while I was eating dinner with my family the next night. I was the only one at the table listening and almost choked.

It would have been the perfect teenage prank. The wire services latched onto the story and it was crawling up the Southeastern United States, into Georgia, Louisiana, Mississippi, Alabama, and South Carolina. But that night Tom went to a party and Lou Walsh, Jr. was there. Tom shot off his mouth about the hoax and it got back to Lou Jr. He confronted Tom, threw a punch at him, and the die was cast. We were screwed. Tom, Earle, and I were haunted by thoughts of prison, years in solitary confinement.

It still baffles me that of the three sets of parents, no one gave a shit. Even George Sr. had to stifle chuckles when Dr. Walsh came over and sat in our living room.

It was like my father was sixteen again, with the sense of humor of his idiot youngest son; we were afraid of looking at each other, afraid of eye-to-eye contact, afraid of an explosion of laughter that would kill the aura of Dr. Walsh's gravity.

He told us how much trouble it was to stop the wire services story, threatened a law suit against us, the Calhouns, the Cortrights, the Miami Daily News, Channel 4, Ralph Rennick, AP, UPI, and Ma Bell, and lamented how our prank had damaged his practice.

XII. U.S. NAVY

I flunked out of high school (actually it was a back seat "oops" but more about that later) and followed Ken into the Navy.

One semester I flunked three high school subjects, chemistry, Spanish, and Algebra II. I was going nowhere, an utter failure primed for mediocrity; a high school dropout, no money, and scared shitless.

Barely seventeen, Navy boot camp in Great Lakes, Illinois was a breeze, as were the Navy crypto and radio intercept schools I was assigned to in Imperial Beach, California. In hindsight, when I left to join the Navy I should have gone to umpire school. Instead of taking the Greyhound to Jacksonville to enlist, I should have taken it to Orlando, to the Jim Evans Professional Umpiring Training Center.

After six years in the Navy and with two older brothers with doctors' degrees, I was under an incredible amount of self-inflicted pressure to get *some* kind of college degree.

I wrote to the Duke Admissions Office, mentioned brothers George Jr. and Ken, described my six years of heroic duty in the U.S. Navy, and asked for undergraduate status. I guess they looked at my high school academic achievements because I never got an answer.

In the Navy my athletic non-accomplishments continued. I played tight end in a military football league in Morocco, North Africa. We were not very good and finished 2-6. In Taipei, Taiwan I played nondescript rugby and fast pitch softball.

I also did a little "boxing" when the Navy communications techs would engage guard company Marines in barracks fistfights. We had three guys who had switched their ratings from aircraft carrier flight deck operations to our communications group; they were mean, tough, and loved to fight. Carrier deck air dales come within feet and seconds of death every time there are flight operations; you learn to stay out of their way.

Guard company Jarheads are mostly dimwits; they're the lowest rung of the Marine Corps.

We had several Marines in our group and they became some of my best friends everywhere I was stationed. And the embassy Marines were also great guys. The Taipei embassy Marines had access to all the booze they wanted and threw a party every Saturday night. All the girls and all the booze you could handle.

One night I hit the sack in one of the many bedrooms of the "Marine House." I was blind drunk and beside me was a beautiful Chinese girl that I could hardly see. I passed out and was awakened several hours later by a Marine groping me. I pushed him away, got up, and returned to my barracks. I told another embassy Marine about the incident and the next time I saw the groper he had been beaten to a pulp.

I didn't like what he had tried to do of course but what his fellow Marines did to him was criminal.

There was kind of a silly indoctrination into manhood whenever the guard company got some kid transferred to them right out of boot camp. To prove his worthiness he had to walk through our barracks, shouting Navy obscenities in the middle of the night. Usually one of our ex-air dales would knock him on his ass and it would start.

XIII. THE OTHER GEORGE

My first father-in-law (another George) was a neat guy. He died twenty-seven years ago and I still miss him. He was the maternal grandfather of my two children. George was a stumpy guy, a plodder with a crooked, swollen nose; an ex-semipro fighter and a Chevrolet assembly-line laborer out of Detroit.

Two years from his end, arthritis was attacking with a vengeance and George's legs were bowed horribly. He gulped aspirin and six-packs to lighten some of the daily suffering.

George taught me how to drink beer: very cold and very fast. On a hot day it was (and still is) the quickest way of getting a cheap buzz.

My wife and I lived with him while I was in college. Fran worked at NSA in Fort Meade, Maryland and with college expenses there was never much money.

George drove a pickup truck and worked the evening shift at a Washington D.C. printing plant. I worked at the local grocery store after classes and would hit the books as soon as I got home. I'd be studying, Fran had gone to bed, and George's headlights would turn into his long driveway. It happened every night; as soon as he got home my studying was complete. He'd walk in with a six-pack of Budweiser "skull-busters" - twenty-four ounce cans shrouded in an ice bag. We would sit in the darkness on his front porch, the living room lamp spilling faded light through the window, gulping skull-busters while he told stories of an earlier life.

One night we took Fran's sister to a frozen lake to ice skate. It was the winter of 1966 and Shirley was 16. Another car pulled up behind George's truck. The driver got out and George, ready to leave, tooted his horn as the man walked away. The man ignored George's horn, words were exchanged, and George and I got out. The man cursed George and then got spilled on his ass from a lightening fast right hand that exploded from the darkness and landed flush on his jaw. I looked at George with my mouth agape, not believing what I had just seen.

"You need to get your hands up," he said to the man as he helped him to his feet.

George was one of the most wonderful people I'd ever met but he was one tough old codger.

I had to get him out of the drunk tank more than once. I'd get a phone call late at night from the Prince George's County police, asking me to come to their barracks and sign for his release. I'd walk back to his cell and he'd be sitting on the cot with blood, dirt, and sometimes vomit on his shirt, the bed, and the floor and with a big grin on his face. The first thing George wanted to do was have a beer. I knew he was close to the end so I would reluctantly look for an open tavern.

I don't think any of us understood his pain and I wish I could live those years over. And I also don't think any of us recognized the extent of his loneliness.

As his arthritis got worse, George retired on disability after fighting Social Security for two years. Divorced, alone, his children gone, and grandchildren who didn't care, George's pain and sadness continued unchecked.

He would drive to a local bar outside of Laurel, Maryland at lunchtime, eat, and start the Budweisers. He would stay until dinner, order, and continue drinking until early in the morning.

Aspirin and Budweiser continued to give him his only pain relief until one night after driving home, he got into bed and died.

He had so much to tell, so much to teach, and so much to give. No one understood the gifts he possessed until it was too late.

XIV. LINGUISTIC SKILLS

I continued various attempts at athletics into my late twenties and early thirties but any skills I had as a teenager eroded quickly. If I wasn't going to make millions as a professional athlete, I still wanted to be close to sports and athletic events and competition. Being an umpire, even a Little League umpire, is the perfect response to that want.

My regret is not getting into umpiring as a young man; had I started the training forty years ago, today I might have at least made some level of professional baseball.

My University of Maryland days were a personal four-year purgatory. After the Navy I established residency in Maryland and perhaps that had something to do with getting accepted at the College Park, Maryland campus. And maybe being six years removed from my high school fiasco helped.

But I got in and somehow swindled a B.A. degree in Secondary Education and hated every second. A couple of times a year I'll still wake up in the middle of the night after a nightmare of having to go back to Maryland, of not having a college degree.

A few years after graduation I was queued in a McDonald's with another insurance agent I worked with, telling him the story of my four semesters of Spanish at College Park.

Krist had his degree from College Park also, having done four years of Adult Education while working for the F.B.I. as a gofer.

"I took an accelerated summer program of two semesters of Spanish between my junior and senior years. My degree demanded four semesters of a foreign language and despite flunking high school Spanish what else was I going to do? Take French? The instructor was a guy about my age and we hit it off immediately. He knew I was married and working full time. He had also served in the military before college so we had a lot to talk about. He gave me an A the first semester, a B the second. But we both knew I was in trouble.

"The regular school year started, I was in my third semester of college Spanish and completely lost. My professor was a very cute Peruvian and I hit on her a number of times, desperate to get on her better side. I had renewed my hatred for Spanish; I couldn't speak it, didn't understand it, couldn't write it, and my Spanish verb conjugation was a source of class delirium."

Krist and I ordered and paid for our food and walked to a booth.

"I guess because I told the professor that she was the most gorgeous woman I'd ever met, she gave me a C and probably wondered how I'd get through my fourth semester of college Spanish.

"My next instructor was a male professor who did not allow English in his classroom. Everyone was fluent and the Spanish jabbering before, during, and after each class was unintelligible and disheartening. Someone would speak to me and I would sheepishly grin and say, 'Si.'

I was graduating soon and *had* to have four passing semesters of Spanish. I knew an *F* was staring me in the face so I went to him and said, 'You're my last hope; I've received an A, a B, and a C. All I need is a D for my diploma. I'll do anything for a D. I'm going to live in North Dakota and I'll never need Spanish. You're the only thing between me and a college diploma; tell you what, if you'll give me a D I'll give you a blow job!' "

Of course that's not what I *really* said but Krist was laughing so hard he dropped his double cheeseburger and spilled his coke.

The bargaining for a D story could also be applied to two other academically impossible courses.

Again, I wish I had used those four years at the University of Maryland to go into formal umpire training. Since graduating forty one years ago, I haven't spent a second in a classroom. I've wasted a lot of time and I've lost too many years of umpiring experience. And I still haven't spoken a word of Spanish.

XV. EARLY LITTLE LEAGUE

I don't remember much about Stephen's Little League years. He did not have a good arm but was truly an all-world defensive catcher and a decent hitter. The other teams ran on him all year and one of the stories I told at his bachelor's party was that the only base stealer he ever threw out was a fat kid who fell down running from first to second. But he could catch anything and *no* one stopped pitches like he did. Little League is two to three hours of wild pitching and poor catching. Most kids don't want to catch; they don't want all that hot and heavy gear on, and they don't want to wear a cup.

Stephen loved catching but he hated the cup. I demanded, begged, cajoled, and threatened; I never thought we had spoiled him but he was stubborn like his mother. I finally gave up, rationalizing that if he was going to enter adulthood ball-less, that it was to be his decision. But he had quick hands, outstanding timing, and feared nothing. He took a lot of hard shots but nothing that damaged anything. He made several swipe tags at home, plays that you just don't see at that level. Behind the plate he was fearless. If only he could have thrown and run.

Our team was OK given my limited baseball knowledge. I wanted the lead runner attacked, no matter what the situation. A kid on second and a hit to the first baseman; if the runner broke,

I wanted him gunned down and to hell with the given out at first. I knew nothing of baseball strategy so any win had nothing to do with my coaching talents.

I loved coaching but wasn't very good at it and got thrown out of a lot of games by pip-squeak teenage umpires who didn't know shit from shinola, who missed calls, and who hated doing my games.

The season was winding down and we were about five and five and playing the league's best team. They were undefeated and had a beast of a player, a college-sized gorilla, twelve-my-ass-years-old, who hit gargantuan shots every at bat.

The Boston Red Sox-Cincinnati Reds World Series had been played five months earlier. The one where with a count of one ball and two strikes on Johnny Bench, runners on second and third and two outs, the Red Sox manager, Darrell Johnson, called time, ambled to the mound, talked briefly to the pitcher, catcher, and infield, and returned to the dugout. Carlton Fisk walked back to the plate and stood, right arm straight out, to accept the beginning pitch of an intentional walk. *Ball Two.* Another lob to the still standing Fisk. *Ball Three.* Bench had long ago relaxed, resting the bat on his massive right shoulder. Now with a full count and Bench ready to trot down to first, the Boston pitcher threw a ninety mile an hour fast ball down the middle. Fisk was still standing when he caught it and Johnny Bench turned to the umpire, opened his mouth as if to protest, thought better of it and walked, head down, back to the Reds' dugout.

If we could somehow get this team into the latter innings with any kind of chance, I was going to pull this same stunt on Gorilla and take away his last at bat. I had a pretty good pitcher going for me and before the game he, Stephen, and I discussed the play. I was not sure that we could pull it off. Even if we could, I had to make sure the pipsqueak umpire would go along. The plate guy didn't like me; he had tossed me before for calling him a name and probably for cursing. Thinking that our pitcher, Stephen, and I were comfortable with the play, I went to the umpire well before the game started and pulled him aside. A manager talking to an umpire before a game starts was nothing out of the ordinary. I revealed our plans and he was okay with everything, probably anxious to witness a play he had never seen. He was doing the whole game by himself, plate, bases, outfield, etc., and I wanted to make sure he was alert when we initiated the deceit. It wasn't as if he was going to forget. It was simple; if we were in the late innings, Gorilla coming to bat, I'd call time, walk to the mound, and it was on.

Anyway, Gorilla *is* at bat, bottom of the fifth and we're leading by a run. A runner on base somewhere and two outs. If we can get the third out, get rid of him as a batter for the rest of the game and then hold on for another inning, we will have beaten the best team in the league, accomplished the impossible, and done something all of us would remember forever.

I call time and walk to the mound, and Stephen comes out, grinning. The count on Gorilla is one and two, the two strikes coming from gigantic shots over the left field fence, both barely foul. The perfect count, the perfect situation, everything perfect. I know the umpire is alert to what's coming but I don't like Stephen's grin and hiss at him. He gets serious and I plead with him not to squat, that if he does, he will give it away. Everyone must think it's an intentional walk and if Stephen squats our ruse will be laid bare.

Ball Two, as my standing son takes the lobbed pitch with his right arm straight out. An intentional walk must be signaled by the catcher standing and not squatting, and with his ungloved hand straight out to his side. Gorilla is fuming and turns to his dad, the coach. Dad shrugs his shoulders and probably thought, "What the heck, two runners, we'll get one or both of them in; we've got some good hitters behind my son." Gorilla is livid; we're taking away his chance of a hit, of driving in the tying run, maybe the go-ahead run. *Ball Three.* Gorilla clinches his jaws in rage and purses his lips, but settles the bat on his shoulder in frustration.

"It might happen, it's working!" I think. We're going to need The Almighty to pull this off, to help us win, and I launch the most reverent prayer I can design, with promises of immeasurable purity in my remaining years.

Then the inexplicable, of course; Stephen *squats* with his right hand still out while Dad screams "*GET READY!*" Stephen had screwed it up, he had done precisely what I had begged him *not* to do, and our hoax is ruined. Providence, however, intervened because just as Dad was figuring things out, our pitcher fired. Gorilla apparently was too mad (or stupid) to unravel the events and stood there dumbfounded as the ball was gunned past him for a called third strike. Gorilla slams the bat into home plate as our team erupts. We gather in the dugout and I announce a pizza party if we can hold on and win. The team goes ape shit.

Well, we *did* win and afterwards gathered at the local Pizza Hut. Two of the fathers and I sat in the dining room drinking beer while the team was put into a back party room. Unbeknownst to us, a food fight breaks out and after it was over I was positive I would be the recipient of a lawsuit. Food was everywhere; pepperoni on the walls, tomato paste splattered against the window, cheese hanging from the ceiling. The grinning twelve members of the Severna Park Yankees were unrecognizable. I apologized profusely to the manager.

"Don't worry about it," he said, "happens all the time."

XVI. UMPIRING 101

It's now two years after the start of my old-age umpiring and maybe I'm as advanced as I'm going to get. I've tried to get beyond Little League, maybe into high school or even the Cal Ripken league but for reasons I do not understand, no one wants me anywhere other than where I am.

For the most part, I love it. I've gone through three umpiring clinics and learned a lot. I've never been a book worm however and reading the damn OFFICIAL REGULATIONS AND PLAYING RULES FOR ALL DIVISIONS OF LITTLE LEAGUE BASEBALL is tortuous.

Here's Rule 6.07 BATTING OUT OF TURN (a):

A batter shall be called out, on appeal, when failing to bat in his/her turn, and another batter completes a time at bat in place of the proper batter. (1) The proper batter may take a position in the batter's box at any time before the improper batter becomes a runner or is put out, and any balls and strikes shall be counted in the proper batter's time at bat. There's (b), (c), and (d) also but if I go much further, I'll begin to nod off like I was sitting in a high school Chemistry class.

Luckily, the real intricate stuff doesn't come up much. When I was a kid, there was Little League, Pony League, Colt League, and American Legion ball. I don't remember all the so-called "divisions" of today's Little League. It starts with Tee Ball, goes to the Minor Division, to the Majors Division, to the Juniors Division, to the Seniors Division, and even to a Big League Little League Division. Each division has age requirements and depending on local needs, skill levels, politics, whatever, one division can meld into another. I would not want to administer any of this; umpiring is as involved as I want to get.

The little guys of Tee Ball scramble all over the field, playing baseball and grab-ass; no one gets put out and a million runs score. It gets a bit less chaotic in the Minor Division and working the plate requires the umpire's normal protective gear. Major Division pitching can be surprisingly strong albeit unpredictable. There are real umpiring problems in this division because the pitchers have advanced more than the catchers for some reason.

I've taken a number of shots simply because a Major Division catcher didn't feel like making an effort to catch a pitch. High and tight to a right-handed batter and I'm in the slot, that open area between the batter and the catcher. The ball comes in, tracking straight for my face mask, nothing between it and me. It takes every fiber of nerve that I have not to spin away.

And before I learned the proper behind-the-plate stance, I got hit on the very top of the head a couple of times. If the umpire's face (and therefore mask) isn't perfectly level, he's asking for trouble. I had a tendency to drop my face just a little. It would barely expose the top of my skull but enough to cause real blood and a lot of pain.

An umpire is supposed to watch the ball into the mitt with just his eyes and no head movement. I still have trouble with a high, tight pitch to a right-handed hitter, maybe because of the experiences of the Majors Division. I tend to back away, an awkward-looking dance step that attempts to mask a flinch. A number of times watching a fast ball railing in high and tight I'll think, "Oh shit, here it comes."

The baselines extend from the sixty feet of the younger divisions to ninety feet in the Junior and older divisions. Our county doesn't have anything higher than Juniors and I've done more Juniors behind the plate than all the other divisions combined. These kids have up to seven or eight years of playing experience and it's a better brand of baseball. Some of the Junior pitchers can throw real heat and an umpire initially thinks he's more exposed to shots. But the catchers have also gotten better and there are not as many passed balls, and they can now block pitches a lot better.

What kills me in all of the divisions is the reluctance to run, especially in the Junior Division when the ball stays in play a lot longer. Kids get on base somehow and there's an inner jubilation. The game and its strategy are forgotten. *"Hooray for me. I'm on first base!"* Meanwhile, the catcher overthrows the pitcher, the ball rolls to center, the shortstop and second baseman are both scratching their asses, and *"Hooray for me"* could be waltzing into second.

Or a kid will draw a walk, trot down to first, touch the base, and take a couple of steps off the bag having gone brain dead. The pitcher is standing twenty feet away, ball in hand, staring at his first baseman and doesn't *do* anything! The batter-runner could be out by twelve feet but is there ever a play made? No; a play would disrupt the order of things and interfere with game harmony.

Maybe it's best this way; the games become predictable and I'm learning what the play's going to be before it takes place. I'm sixty-eight and whereas I used to have no speed, I now have the added burden of thirty-five extra pounds. But speed to me is not critical. Positioning is and the predictability makes positioning easy. Add a rotting left hip and I pretty much stay glued to whatever piece of turf I'm occupying at the moment.

At my first clinic, there are maybe twenty students, most of them in their teens to mid-twenties. A couple of guys in their forties or fifties, but they were the instructors. I'm the oldest one in the class and Mac, our district umpiring chief, tells us we should always run a few sprints before each game to loosen up and to demonstrate umpiring mobility to everyone. To start the clinic, he orders us to sprint to the fence and back, maybe a total of one hundred yards. All the young bucks take off, and I too limp away. Every kid passed me going the opposite way. Mac's a good guy but stern and demanding. He merely frowned as I crawled back.

Mac has chewed my ass a number of times. To a fan, even to a coach or player, I run a good game. I keep things moving and my game is typically over an inning or so sooner than an adjacent game. I stay alert and stay on top of everything. I used to pull scabs out of the stands to do the bases. I'd look at some father sitting in the stands, walk up to the fence and say, "Do you know anything about baseball?"

"No way, man." or "Well, I've played some as a kid."

Some of them worked out okay, most didn't. I soon learned that I could control games better by just doing everything myself. Again, ninety-nine percent of it is predictability and positioning. At the pre-game plate meeting with the managers I'll say something like, "If it's a judgment call, don't even bother. I'm by myself and I'm not going to change anything. If I've screwed up a rule, come on out; but if it's a judgment play keep your asses parked."

XVII. LITTLE LEAGUE SURVIVAL

In Little League baseball there's an axiom that must be followed if you're to survive as an umpire: *FIND* strikes and outs. The strike zone gets extended from the ears to the ankles and if it's close, he's out. The best thing you can say about a Little League baseball game you've just umpired is that it's over. As the innings drag on you want it to end. Around the fourth or fifth inning, especially on a hot day, I'll be dying for a cold beer. The next day, however, I'm ready to go again.

I'm not sure why but I lose the balls and strikes count, even with my indicator. I don't think it's always my fault ... a lot of time the electronic scoreboard disagrees with my numbers. I call time and turn around and ask for confirmation. I do it so as not to disrupt the flow of the game. It bothers me that some big white numbers 200 feet away don't agree with my indicator. Mac saw this happen a number of times and called my cell phone one night at home. "The next time I see you ask the scorekeeper for the count, I'm going to yank your ass out of umpiring, gawdammit!"

And I'm left-handed, mostly. I write, throw, and eat left-handed. Making an out call demands a right-handed arm pump, something like striking a nail with a hammer, with the fist and forearm finishing vertical. I make left-handed out calls. Another call one night: "The next time I see you make a left-handed out call, I'm going to yank your ass out of umpiring, gawdammit! Take your left hand and tie it to your fucking pecker!"

After each game I add to an umpiring diary on my laptop. I summarize the game, make note of any close calls, recite any interesting and/or outstanding plays, and grade myself. In the early part of the year a lot of the notes have to do with quality of play. These kids today spend too much time on their computers, too much time texting each other, too much time playing video games, too much time on electronic gadgetry.

XVIII. UMPIRING DIARY

One night I pulled Alan from the stands to do the bases. One of the coaches had a son on his team, a nice enough kid but somewhat of a sass. There was a play at second involving the kid and Alan makes a bad call. After the inning he discussed the play with me and told me the kid had cursed him, an offense that demands automatic ejection. But I hadn't heard it and let it go. An inning later the same kid is on third and comes home on a close play. I thumb him out and he comes out of his slide fuming. He mumbles something I don't hear while going to his dugout and turns and stares at me. I follow him the rest of the way and at the dugout gate I put a finger in his face and say, "Don't make me toss you." Two outs later he comes to bat asking, "Blue, how many outs?"

"Two."

"Two! How'd you get *two?*"

"Ralph, shut up and get in the box."

He works the count full and I ring him up on a ball that was in the dirt and eight inches outside. *Never* show up an umpire.

I think it was in this game that I took my first scalp shot, one that actually drew blood. The next day I went to a Fort Myers umpire equipment store and bought a batting helmet and had a cage attached. Now I could do all the flinching I wanted! But the helmet was too hot in the South Florida heat and I went back to a regular mask. Besides, I was afraid the helmet would instill some bad habits … like flinching.

Every once in awhile I'll be facing some 6-2, sixteen year old, who's throwing fire. At sixteen a lot of these kids are still just rearing back and throwing with as much velocity as they can. They haven't learned how to throw breaking stuff, how to be crafty, how to set up batters. A couple of pitches at eighty-five miles an hour and I might start losing my umpiring nerve. I have to fight it because I can be tempted to throw my mask up in the air, walk to a dugout, and yell, "Enough! I'm not going to do this anymore!" But I don't because I love the game and I love the challenge that umpiring presents.

And I guess I love the kids … most of them. The majority are obedient, honest, and anxious to get better. The Latinos are a pleasure to umpire. In the Minors and Majors they bring superior skills and baseball knowledge. They're polite, never question an umpire's call, and return to the dugout without a hint of protest on a called third strike. They throw, hit, catch, and run better than the other kids.

It changes in the Juniors however. The Caucasians (and the occasional black) seem to grow bigger faster than the Latinos. And even though they both have progressed through Tee Ball (ages 4-6), Minors (ages 7-9), and Majors (ages 10-12), and have eight years of playing experience, the white kids seem to be stronger and able to drive the ball harder. There are good Latinos in the Juniors, but the majority of the really skilled players are the white kids.

The local high school football coach has a little boy who plays in the Major Division. The father is about my size but a lot younger and a lot more muscular. His little boy is smaller than every kid on the field and as cute as he can be. Fred wants him to be a catcher but I'm not sure the coach wants him to be a catcher. In the games he *does* catch, I'm worried about the little guy. But he's not bad and it surprises me how tough he is. He handles heat as well as any catcher in the division but like a lot of young catchers, he hasn't developed any arm strength. He'll get bigger and stronger, but after the season's last game I was talking to his father and he said, "He has a very good stroke and a decent eye but he's oh for the freekin' season."

XIX. THE LAKE PLACID YEARS

My timing skills developed, I believe, as a youngster. Our family starting vacationing in Lake Placid, Florida in 1949. As kids, Ken and I used to take our .22 caliber Remington target shooting.

When I was around ten we were at the county dump looking for rats or anything else that moved. A lone crow drifted from our left to right, maybe one hundred yards out, thirty feet above the mounds of garbage, its wings rotating slowly. I pulled the rifle to my shoulder while Ken mumbled, "No way." I mentally calculated the needed lead, moved the barrel accordingly, and pulled the trigger. The .22 round struck, staggered the bird, and it began tumbling to earth as Ken gasped, "GAWWW!" We were astonished when it regained its aerodynamics and continued on.

Another time we were in front of our lake cabin. Ken had the gun and took aim at a crow perched thirty yards away on a pine tree limb. He fired and the crow flew to the ground among thick palmetto bushes. "I got him!" Ken said as we raced through the palmettos. I knew better but helped him look anyway. A little later I shot a crow about the same distance in another pine tree. The passerine plunged tail first, one broken wing protruding awkwardly. We found him flopping around and I administered the coup de grace. Athletically, I've always had decent accuracy and I suppose that and timing are essential to my umpiring.

A lot of central Florida woodland isn't woodland at all; it's palmetto bushes and an occasional Sabal palm or scrub pine. The panoramas are forever, vast acreages of two foot high palmettos, heat waves dancing off the brush, and usually a fresh water lake in view.

I remember wondrous days walking down the dirt road next to Lake Placid in our bare feet, wearing nothing but a pair of shorts. The hot Florida sun baking our already dark skins, sweat cascading off of our trim torsos, not a shade tree in sight, crickets singing, Florida jays fussing, and the crystal clear fresh water of Lake Placid beckoning. We'd see an opening in the palmettos from the dirt road to the sandy shoreline and sprint for the white sand beach and the cool lake water.

Lake Placid lake is three and one half miles from end to end and two miles across. Ken and I swam, skied, and fished every single day.

One day we discovered a small cove off the western side of the lake, about a mile from our cabin. My dad had bought us an eighteen foot fiber glass boat with a seventeen horse Mark 20 Mercury outboard motor.

The Mark 20 was a trolling motor compared to today's monsters, but Ken and I could nevertheless ski behind it.

The cove was hidden from the shoreline by wild Bougainvilleas, its entrance completely camouflaged. On this day we were crawling along the shoreline, trolling for bass when Ken saw something. We reeled in our lures and he steered around a Bougainvillea point and suddenly, we were in a different world. To this day I honestly believe we were the first (or some of the first) humans to witness the awesome beauty of the tiny inlet. There was no evidence that anyone had been there before; no trash, no beer cans, no cigarette butts. The cove was tiny but deep and swarming with Bluegills, large oak trees formed a dense canopy, and thick brush surrounded us.

The cove belonged to Ken and me and we never told a soul about it. It was 1950 and shoreline development around the big lake was a dozen cabins and an old resort three miles away. Maybe some Indians several centuries before had fished the cove, but certainly not recently.

Ken and I would get up very early and with rods, reels, and fat blood worms, make our way to our cove. Within an hour we had enough Bluegills on our gill line to feed the entire family. Ken and I would filet the fish and our father would fry them in butter with eggs and cook a pot of grits.

XX. MAC, UMPIRE-IN-CHIEF

My first umpiring clinic in January of 2009 was mostly administrative stuff in the morning session; the pre-game meeting, proper conduct, proper dress, rosters, game control, proper slotting (positioning), etc. In the afternoon we worked on making calls and then we each had a turn behind the plate.

We had been told to bring ALL of our gear, that we'd be behind the plate calling balls and strikes. I was the only student wearing shin protectors, mask, and a vest. They set up a pitching machine and had a little kid, in full catcher's gear, taking the throws. I winced time and again as the ball streamed in, hit the kid someplace other than his glove, and bounce away. I didn't understand how he was taking all those shots without any visible reaction. I soon realized why no one else was wearing their equipment and why the kid wasn't getting hurt. The balls were powder-puffs, pillowy things that were soft as marshmallows. I was a bit embarrassed as I took my turn behind the plate, fully protected, listening to the giggles of the other students.

Mac was running the clinic and I've since wondered if he doesn't deliberately snooker me. A couple of times I've gotten calls from him.

"Mike, can you do a *Seniors* game in Lehigh tomorrow night?"

"Seniors? Is there some Senior ball in Lehigh?" You would think that after the first time I would have figured it out. Lehigh is a seventy mile roundtrip drive and doing a Seniors game is about the only reason I'd want to drive that far. Well the "Seniors" turned out to be Girls' Senior Fast Pitch softball.

In my defense the second time it happened was after Mac had chosen me for all-star postseason tournament play. I felt, given his ass-chewings during the season, rather proud of myself and it flew right over me again when he announced a "Seniors game in Lehigh."

Actually, girls' fast pitch isn't all that bad. Basically it's baseball rules and it can get fun when the pitchers can throw heat. Lee County has a very competitive girls' program and us District 18 umps are expected to do our share of those games. I don't mind doing them as long as they'll continue to let me do the Majors and Juniors.

After a year of experience and three clinics I began to think of getting into more advanced stuff, if nothing more than local Little League World Series district and State tournament games. As I said before, I'm not sure it's ever going to happen.

After getting picked for tournament play, I did two postseason World Series regional games, one the plate, the other the bases, and Mac hasn't called me since.

Thankfully, he didn't watch the plate game because I lost the count a dozen times. We had done a recent clinic of the umps that were chosen to do tournament games. Keep in mind that most of my stuff is behind the plate and by myself with an occasional scab doing the bases. I've learned how to rotate a two-man crew and can easily adapt to whatever another umpire wants to do. I consider myself still inexperienced and still learning, and if I'm doing a plate game with someone who is senior to me I'll acquiesce to his rotations. Some guys want the entire infield to themselves, some want the plate guy to cover third, some want a rotation of the plate to third depending on the play, and there are different versions of who covers the outfield, who calls fair-foul, etc. Of course, with the scabs, I do it *my* way.

At this clinic, Mac announces that all tournament games will be with the plate guy and *two* base umpires, a three-man crew. A three-man system is a whole new world and there are a lot of plays that rotate differently than anything I had seen. I sweat out the clinic and go home and study and restudy the rotations. Mentally, I'm okay with a three-man but I'm worried if I can manage a game without botching something.

Another long drive to Lehigh and I'm floored when it's announced that Roy and I are doing a two-man. Roy is an EMT in real life, has about the same experience as me, carries himself with the aplomb of a Major Leaguer, and is going to be a very good umpire.

It is my first all-star game, the one in which I kept losing the count. But again, a lot of it is simply the scoreboard count not agreeing with my hand-held indicator. Sometimes, you've got some kid back there working the scoreboard who's daydreaming and who's a pitch (or two) behind. Usually, the official scorekeeper is somewhat experienced. The two sit side-by-side in an elevated booth directly behind the plate and the fence.

I see a disparity and turn to the scorekeeper once again with "What's the count?"

"Two and two."

"I've got two and one."

"Two and two."

Roy was using his own indicator which a base umpire is *not* supposed to do. I wave him in from his C position (somewhere between the shortstop and second base).

"Roy, I've got two and one; what do you have?"

"Two and one."

I turn to the scorekeeper and announce, "Two and one; change the board."

"No. Tina said I have final say."

Tina is a cute 35 year old who runs everything there is to run in Southwest Florida Little League Baseball. She was at the site but apparently watching another game at an adjacent field. I guess my scorekeeper had spoken to her about the lost counts. I look at Roy, frowning, and he looks at the scorekeeper and says, "*That* is *never* going to happen; change the damn board."

Umpires are God at the site of a Little League game. No one, *No One* has more authority than a Little League plate umpire at game site. We can toss a player, a coach, a head coach, a fan, even another umpire. A plate umpire (an umpire in chief) has supreme authority. I saw an Internet story recently whereby a Little League umpire tossed the entire seating section of the home team. The plate umpire *must* control the game, and anything that disrupts his ability to do so can get heaved.

I had been scheduled to do the next night's game at the same site and after we finished the scorekeeper hunts me down and announces gleefully that I've been pulled.

I have hip replacement surgery coming up and after this game I had trouble even walking. My left hip is quickly decomposing. I usually recover the next day, enough to even umpire again, but this game was particularly punishing.

These kids have as much chance of going to the World Series as they do of making the Major Leagues but until their team has been eliminated, it's a time when life itself hangs in the balance. The coaches are substituting everyone, every position, every pitcher, every inning. I can usually get these games over in less than two hours ... easily. This one was two and one half hours and I thought it was a night without end.

XXI. THE CRISCO KID

The next day I emailed Mac and described the count meeting between the scorekeeper, Roy, and me. I knew he would be mad but I also wanted to confirm that I had been pulled. He knows about my surgery and of course has seen me hobble around a baseball field many times. His reply was simply that I was doing the bases with Jose de la Chico in Bonita next Thursday night. I *had* been pulled.

My diary has an entry that reads, "Maybe I should just stick with the local stuff and not worry about post season or advancing up the umpiring ladder."

Jose is a fat little Mexican from Immokalee, a former Indian reservation about 35 miles east of Fort Myers. It's a small town that's home to southwest Florida's farm workers and a Seminole Indian casino. The Mexican immigrants have overrun the place and the Seminoles have fled back to the Everglades.

That Jose would be picked to do all-star tournament stuff is testament to Mac's sense of equality and fair play. I met him (I call him "Crisco" in my diary) in the umpire's room before the game for the first time. I'm only 5-9 and towered several inches over him. He wore non-regulation pants, a stained white t-shirt, and filthy shoes. Crisco buckled on his shin guards *over* his pants and tugged a dirty umpire's shirt over his vest.

I always go to the game wearing shined shoes and regulation (and clean) pants and shirt. I may not be any good but I want to *look* good.

The undershirt color is supposed to match the sleeve piping on the umpire's shirt because it shows at the open neck. So if the umpires are wearing a Carolina blue shirt with red piping, the color of their undershirts are red. We're wearing Carolina blue and Crisco's T-shirt is dirty white.

I also shower and shave before each game. Crisco has a two-day growth of ugly facial hair and smells like a maggot. **Where do they get these guys?**

I've heard that if Little League officials are grading an umpire, his appearance counts more than his ability to get calls right.

I was almost embarrassed to walk onto the field with Crisco. He had been a half hour late so I had completed the pre-game ritual of checking each dugout's bats and helmets for irregularities. We passed through one of the dugouts together and entered the field, Crisco to the applause of several of his Mexican buddies standing outside the fence.

He conducted the plate meeting and did not introduce anyone to anyone. Protocol says introduce the two coaches to each other and to all of the umpires, review any local field nuances, do the line-up reviews, and ask each coach if his players understand the rules and regulations of *XYZ* division Little League baseball and if they're properly equipped according to the rules and regulations of *XYZ* division Little League baseball. You *must* demand a *yes* answer, nothing more, nothing less. The coaches quickly learn that flippant answers are not acceptable. "I think so" means the question gets asked again. It gets asked again and again until you get a "yes."

The "yes" requirement is to reduce Little League's liability exposure. If a kid gets his testicles shoved into his throat by a fastball it's no longer our fault. I used to go so far as to demand a "cup knock." The catchers respond to "Lemme hear it" automatically and tap a fist against their cup. As things get refined

I've pretty much done away with the "knock" request. I did it at first but the senior umpires don't do it.

"Dooo yooo haf dee lineups? Dey loooook hoookay. Les gooo."

Usually after the plate meeting the umpires will confer about rotation and coverages. There are three slots or positions of base umpires, A, B, and C. A is along the foul line behind first base with no runners on. B is near second base with a runner on first, coverage that gives the umpire good angles at both second and first base, and the C slot is somewhere near the shortstop *usually* taken with runners on second and/or third. C is the toughest slot in my opinion because first base is still that umpire's responsibility and on the ninety foot fields, it's a mile away. Using a two-man, the base umpire usually utilizes all the slots, depending on where the runners are.

"Jose, how do you want me to rotate?"

"Eeeny way."

"Well, do you want me to cover all the bases?"

"Noooo, Ah'll dooo tird."

"OK; then I should not be in the C slot even with a runner on second?"

"Si…Yes. Yoooooooo shud."

"So from the C position, you don't want me to call anything at third?"

"If yoooo clos eeenough."

One of the purposes of the C slot is to *be* close enough.

I knew further discussion would be brainless so we get the game going when he yells, "PLAAAAY!" (I learned early in my umpiring career that "Play *Ball!*" went out with the rotary phone.)

The first thing that happened was a bonehead play I called at first base from the C position. There was a runner at third and the ball was hit to the shortstop. The shortstop threw to first and the first baseman caught the ball and fired to home trying to nab the runner sliding into the plate. I thought he pulled his foot off first base and after hesitating (just for a couple of seconds … as you're *supposed* to), screamed "Safe! He pulled his foot!" I still think it was the proper call but one that should never be made. Mac says, "If you need a slow-motion camera, forget it." In Little League baseball, remember, an umpire looks for outs, he manufactures outs, he designs outs. If you don't call outs, the game never ends. Anyway, the Crisco Kid then does something that also should never happen.

Judgment calls are protected in baseball circles like the Crown Jewels; they are the umpire's exclusive right and are defended to the death. If there are six umpires, seventy thousand fans, and two billion TV viewers who see a play as an out but if the responsible umpire calls "Safe," the safe stands. An umpire may ask for help if he was out of position or for any other reason, but once the call is made it's supposed to stick. For Jose to question one of my judgment calls is also to question my character, my dignity, my honesty, my manhood.

Now comes the Crisco Kid waddling out to the infield. I don't like what I'm seeing but earlier in a regular season game, the same thing happened, the results got heated, and I want to avoid that type of scene in postseason tournament play.

"Eeet was a baaad cah."

"Jose, the kid pulled his foot," I answer, now knowing the safe call should not have been made.

"Eeet was a baaad cah."

"OK, you're the umpire-in-chief; do you want to change it?"

"I wa' yooou to change eeet."

"Jose, the other coach will go ballistic. If the call is going to be changed, *you're* going to change it."

"OK; heee out!" he yells turning away. I was surprised when the other coach did nothing; maybe because at the time he was leading 5-0.

Again from the C slot. A play at third and the throw beats the runner easily but the third baseman doesn't get the tag down. Umpires, especially Little League umpires, call automatic outs if the gloved ball is simply dropped to the ground between the bag and the sliding runner. It doesn't matter if an actual tag is made, only that the placement of the glove is done properly. "Safe!" I yell, immediately regretting it.

Here comes The Kid again, this time with his chubby right arm raised, thumb out.

"Eeet was a baaad cah."

Enough's enough.

"Jose, it was *not* a bad call. The kid didn't get the tag down."

"Oookay," he says and walks away.

Later, a close play at first for a game-ending double play. I got it right and head for the winning dugout as the players pile out and high-five one another. *Always* exit through the winning dugout with your fellow umpire(s); why subject yourself to the scorn of the losers? The Kid doesn't exit but hangs out in the infield, in front of the losing dugout, where his buddies have gathered. I hear some very fast, very excited Spanish and wonder if they're talking about my calls.

XXII. NEIGHBORS, SHOTS, AND FELLOW UMPIRES

A couple of nights later I sat in the stands with my wife Barb and watched a Major Division championship International postseason all-star game between the local San Carlos team and a team from Fort Myers Beach. This stuff is "international" only because if a U.S. team keeps winning, it gets into THE Little League World Series game against a team from the international bracket. The local kids aren't that good; no team is going beyond another game or two.

Ike Patterson, a tall good-looking nineteen year old, is doing the plate and is considered one of our senior umpires. Despite his youth, Ike's been doing Little League umpiring four years.

Brett Mayer is in the A slot and another short, fat Mexican is on the third base line. Brett is also a VERY senior umpire but won't do the plate. He's probably older than me and is very cocksure, a very good thing to be while umpiring.

Ike has a *presence* I wish I could copy. Behind the plate, he rises to the extent of his 6-3 height and bellows, "STREEEE!" throwing his right fist towards the pitcher. We're taught proper pitch-calling mechanics but it's understood that being unique is acceptable. I stand and point down the first base line and call something like "HOO-A." I've learned that the louder my "HOO-A," the less bitching I get.

One of my neighbors' kid, Matt, got picked for the San Carlos all-star team. He's a real good kid, the same age as my grandson, Michael, and has decent skills.

His father, Matt Sr. however, rides his mistakes unmercifully.

Matt Jr. plays shortstop and pitches. It was a tight game and near the end, Matt's coach moves him from shortstop to pitcher. I lean over to Barb, "Watch out; he's going to get shelled." I had done a couple of his pitching games during the regular season, mostly relief appearances, and knew he didn't have much velocity. At this age, velocity can make a kid all-world. Without velocity and without yet having learned to throw breaking stuff, pitching becomes *a who-can-throw-it-over-the-plate?* farce.

Fort Myers Beach starts teeing off on Matt and a 3-2 game goes quickly to 8-2. I glance at Matt Sr. His face has darkened, his eyes are slit half-closed, his jaw locked in silent rage. I feel sorry for his boy.

In a regular season game with his kid throwing to everything *but* the catcher, Matt Sr. sat in the stands screaming, "You're throwing like a girl!" After a couple of these putdowns I walk over to the fence between innings and motion him toward me. He steps down.

"Matt, cool it. I can't let you do that. It's only Little League, for crap's sake."

"OK," he replies and returns to his seat and shuts up.

Later, Matt is the first batter of the inning and the pitcher is still throwing warm-ups.

"Your father really gets into it, doesn't he?"

"He's a pain in my ass," he answers softly.

I've seen Ike do a number of plate games. I am baffled how he never seems to take shots. He has a good stance, everything about it is correct except his hands. Both of his hands are exposed as the pitch comes in. I've noticed that a lot of Major League umpires also seem to expose their hands. Ike bends his knees properly and also bends properly from the waist. But being as tall as he is and with a very wide stance, he places each hand on an exposed knee. I keep one hand behind the catcher and the other, the one exposed by the slot, behind my shin guard-protected knee.

Umpires take shots all the time; it's an accepted part of baseball. We wear vests, masks, cups, sometimes helmets, and shin guards that cover our knees, shins, ankles, and feet. And steel-toed shoes. Some guys wear bicep pads and I guess there's other padding as well.

I've taken shots on every inch of my body I think. I took a shot directly to my cup one night and groaned as I spun away. The catcher found it amusing and laughed but professionally called time and walked to the mound to allow me recovery time.

When a Major Division catcher doesn't stop a fast ball and it hits me square, my mask gets knocked cockeyed. Umpires wear their masks loose; a tight-fitting mask will transfer the shock of a fast ball, a loose mask dissipates it.

I love the scene. An old guy doing the plate, gets nailed and staggers away. You'd be surprised at the empathy that rolls out of the stands. And I milk it, feigning mortal injury. It's one of my ways to get the crowd behind me no matter how crappy my calls.

"You OK, Blue?" will come a call from the stands. Bent over, my hands on my knees, head down in alleged agony, I'll raise one hand. One night after a particularly dramatic response, a guy in the stands yells, "He's a tough old bird." I rose, grinned, and did a Tiger Woods fist pump.

Brett, the guy in the A position, the guy who won't do the plate, made some good, tight calls and got them right. I complimented him after the game. With three umpires, he never had to take the C position. The fat little Mexican could have slept through the entire game and maybe he did. I don't think he made one call all night.

That can happen with a three or more-man crew. If I ever got in World Series stuff, it would be at least four-man, probably six.

Doing games with just one base umpire or by myself is very demanding. One second, *one second,* of drifting thoughts and you can miss a critical part of the game. You *must* stay on top of everything and you must do it uninterrupted for two hours. You're involved in every play, every pitch, every second. I once told Stephen, "The best position in baseball is catcher. You're involved in *everything.*" So too with plate umpiring.

XXIII. FALL BALL

Between "Fall Ball" (an autumn practice league) and early March, Florida concentrates on the Gators, Seminoles, Hurricanes, Dolphins, Buccaneers, and Jaguars. But Little League cranks up again after only a three month respite.

Of course I've come to know all of the local head coaches. Some of them are very good, some should run the concession stand. A lot of these guys accompany their own kids through the Little League years and you never see them again. As it should be I suppose, but I enjoy the guys who are really into coaching; they know baseball and they love teaching it. Their kids have grown up and left but they're still giving their time, work, and money to Little League. The good ones use Fall Ball only as a training and learning schedule, not really caring about game scores. Mike and Hewell are two of the good ones. Neither of them cares about a game's outcome; only that their players are learning.

Hewell is a rules guru. I think he knows more about the PLAYING RULES than most of the umpires in our district and he's not above helping an inexperienced umpire. He's losing by a couple of runs late in the game and I think I see his pitcher balk. With a runner on third, a balk will score a run. I call time and wave him from the dugout.

"Hewell, I think your pitcher just balked. Before I call it I wanted to verify it."

"Really? I didn't see anything; wha'd he do?"

"I don't think he came to a complete stop."

"OK; call it. But I wanna talk to my pitcher."

I wave the runner in and Hewell goes to the mound to discuss the infraction with his pitcher.

This is what Fall Ball should be.

On the other hand some coaches use Fall Ball to practice ineptness, to demonstrate stupidity, to rehearse coach-umpire conflicts.

One October afternoon game Tom storms out of his dugout. "Blue, get in the damn game!" he yells knowing the informality of Fall Ball diminishes the chance of getting heaved for light swearing. I *am* into the game but I've enlarged the strike zone as the innings begin to pile up.

In the regular season a "Damn" is supposed to get the coach heaved and "Fuck" might be grounds for prison. I mean some of these kids are *doing* it but using the F word is an absolute travesty on the dignity of Little League baseball.

I've read Major League baseball accounts of managers going ballistic and the more original the swearing, the more the umpires enjoy it.

"Tom, arguing balls and strikes is an automatic ejection," I grin.

"But stuff in the dirt shouldn't be strikes, for crissakes!"

"Hey, we're pushing two hours; do you want the lights on?"

"No but I want my guys to learn the strike zone, gawdammit!"

He had a point but it was taking too much time to teach them.

XXIV. MAKE THE CALL

Because I'm deaf in my right ear, at my plate meetings I sometimes add: "I'm hard of hearing; if you call 'Time' or 'Blue' and I don't respond it's not because I don't like you. Just keep yelling and I'll eventually recognize you."

Some umpires, on real close plays, make safe-out decisions based on sound. The sound of the ball hitting the first baseman's mitt versus the sound of the batter-runner's foot reaching the bag. I've tried but can't do it. I'll pick up the fielder's throw while watching the batter-runner peripherally and time the result. I think I'm good at making safe-out calls but I react too quickly.

Good umpiring says watch the play, think about the result, then make the call. But the Major League umpires make calls very differently. On a very easy play, say where the throw beats the batter runner to first by a mile, the umpire gets in position, watches, and long after the play is over, slowly raises his arm and fist for the out call. But on a close play, the call is immediate and I sometimes wonder if they don't have it reversed. But I find myself doing the same thing. I guess being fast on a close play implies to the rest of the park that you got it right.

It's the same with balls and strikes: watch, think, make the call.

One night I was doing the plate in a Juniors game and Kevin, a very senior, experienced, and good umpire has the bases. After the game we meet and discuss my game. "Mike, your balls and strikes are right on but you're yelling 'Strike' while the ball's still in the air. At least wait until it hits the glove." It's all part of the learning curve; I'm trying to slow down.

On base plays, my *timing* allows me to make a call the instant the play happens and there's no thinking, waiting, and making a call ten seconds after the play is over. My instant calls have been the subject of one of Mac's ass-chewings. I may get my ass chewed but no one complains that my calls are wrong. Even on a ninety-foot field from the C position and not able to race closer to the play as you're supposed to, I can use my timing to make accurate calls. I miss calls, we all do. I just don't think I need to be a 20-year old speedster to be a decent Little League umpire.

XXV. THE GAMES AND THE GUNS

Today, Lake Placid hasn't changed much from the 1950s. Lot prices have sky-rocketed but aside from more development around the shoreline of the various lakes, the little town is the same. The adjacent north-south highway, U.S. 27, has seen a lot of fast-food growth but the main street, east-west Interlake Boulevard, is as asleep as it was in 1952.

You could have bought a lakefront half-acre lot back then for $500, but today you might pay half a million. I've always loved central Florida but the fresh water lakes with sugary sand, gentle slopping shorelines, and huge bass attract few tourists.

Our family started vacationing in Lake Placid in 1949. The three hour 150 mile drive up U.S. 27 from Miami was monotonous and sometimes filled with adventure.

The highway angled northwest out of Miami, in and out of South Bay, Clewiston, Moore Haven, and into Lake Placid and beyond. It skirted Lake Okeechobee, Seminole Indian reservations, and vast tracts of the blackest earth I'd ever seen. Sugar cane thrived here, and still does, but I *still* don't know how earth can be that black.

My father never made much money but he always drove big cars. I don't know how he afforded them, maybe by our family's deprivation. We didn't have much and I suspect that only my mother's salary as a Dade County school registrar kept us afloat (and my dad in new cars). The family would pile into his new 1953 air-conditioned Oldsmobile 98 and take off.

The "games" usually started south of South Bay. Black teenagers with nothing better to do, driving jalopies, would race up behind my dad, begin to pass him, come along beside him laughing, cursing, and giving him the finger. The game required them to slow down in front of us, making my dad pass them. This might go on for most of the fifty mile stretches of empty highway, a new Oldsmobile 98 and a jalopy leapfrogging back and forth.

As little kids, my brothers and I were scared senseless. It was the black kids' version of *chicken* but really angered no one but my father.

On long lonely stretches of highway he would sometimes let me drive. I'd sit on a cushion, barely reaching the brake pedal and accelerator, with my face angled upward to see above the steering wheel. I had not mastered the art of steering a car and as the Olds would begin to drift, I'd yank it back ... but too far and yank it again. We would zigzag down the highway, me trying to keep the Oldsmobile on the road while my father belly-laughed.

One day we were driving up by ourselves and it started. We had just changed places again and he was behind the wheel ... thankfully. An old Hudson Hornet pulled up beside my father and the black teenager in the passenger seat grinned at my father and cursed him.

"Fuckin' niggers," he said and reached across me, opened the glove box, and yanked out a .38 Smith and Wesson short-barreled handgun.

He used the *N* word all the time but it was the first time I think he had used the *F* word in front of one of his sons.

He rolled down his window and pointed the gun straight at the black teenager in the front passenger seat and cocked the hammer. My dad and the kid were side by side at sixty miles an hour, the muzzle about three feet from the teenager's nose. The glee on the poor kid's face changed to horror, the frown on my dad's to a big grin. I heard the weird clanking of old brake shoe and drum assemblies as the Hornet nose-dived, jerked in behind us, and disappeared never to bother us again.

On another occasion it started south of Lake Placid. We turned left onto Florida Highway 70 assuming the black kids would continue north. We had another five miles before Placid View, the dirt road north to our lake cabin.

"Dad! They're still there!" I said, turning in my seat, watching them wheel in behind us.

"I know," he said calmly. "The rifle's in the trunk. I'll stop after we're on Placid View. If they turn in behind us, shoot the bastards." I was scared and dumbfounded but we had turf to defend and defend it we would. He accelerated the Olds to put some distance between us and our pursuers and whipped into Placid View throwing up storms of dust. We continued about fifty yards and he slammed on the brakes, grabbed his .38, ordered me out, unlocked the trunk, and handed me the Remington. My dad was on the right side of the Olds and I'm hunched next to the left quarter panel trying not to wet myself, the dust still swirling. My dad was in the classic handgun shooters stance, feet apart, the .38 in his right hand, right arm fully extended, and his left hand palming his right.

"I'm twelve years old and getting ready to get into a gunfight," I think. I'm sure our adversaries had Thompsons and .50 caliber machine guns and after an exchange of gunfire, the Oldsmobile, my dad, and I would be riddled to pieces. I am therefore in my own version of surrender with my arms hanging down, my hands cradling the rifle.

"Goddamnit, get ready!" he growls and I reluctantly shoulder the Remington and swing the barrel toward Florida Highway 70. The black kids turn in behind us and seeing two people aiming loaded guns their way, jam on the brakes, start sliding on the loose dirt, and come to a stop ten feet from the muzzles of the .38 Smith and Wesson and the .22 Remington.

I remember how suddenly *everything* came to a halt, even the earth itself. There was no sound, no movement, nothing; it was a terrifying standoff and I was frightened shitless but the windshield, the steering wheel, and the kid driving the jalopy were nevertheless right in the middle of my gun sight.

I was very worried about the teenagers jumping out of their car, guns blazing, so if the kid in my sights even moved, I was going to begin yanking the trigger. I was going to die but I was going to take the black teenager with me. The kid slowly raised one hand as if pleading, ground the jalopy into reverse, backed slowly onto Florida Highway 70, his eyes never leaving me and the Remington and raced away. I still don't know why my father did not begin firing but I was thankful he didn't.

Florida was a different place back then.

XXVI. BUZZARDS AND MORE BUZZARDS

Roland Sharp was a high school chum and he occasionally accompanied us to the cabin for long weekends. Roland and I would walk down Placid View with the Remington, looking for trouble, and firing at anything that moved. Roland was my height but substantially overweight. My dad loved to tease him because Roland would lose his smile, redden with embarrassment, and lower his head. It was a reaction my father loved to invoke.

A buzzard lolled overhead and I took aim. They were easy targets especially when they were low. Just a bit of a lead and we could hear the impacts of the semi-automatics. But they have a very thick layer of feathers and after staggering in mid-air, they would continue on. Whether they later dropped out of the sky I never knew. I did know that I had never knocked one out of the air.

One summer, after my family had moved from Miami to Lake Placid, Earle, Tom, and Roland drove up for a weekend. We were high school juniors and into cars, girls, and beer. On Saturday night we went to a party, drank a few beers, and got bored. My buddies knew no one and I knew very few. Tom and I left around midnight looking for something else to do. Earle and Roland stayed at the party and we told them we'd be back in a couple of hours. Roland sucked draft beer, got into chugging contests with a couple of Sebring kids and won two bucks.

Meanwhile, Earle hooked up with a pretty sophomore and eventually conned her to the backyard and there, concealed by tall Hibiscus shrubs, further conned her out of her panties.

We reconvened and stumbled home at two in the morning.

That day one of my father's rancher friends had invited us onto his spread to go catfishing. My dad made the best catfish chowder in the world, spicy and served over Spanish yellow rice. He promised to cook a batch if we'd filet anything we caught.

Summer rains had saturated central Florida that year. The rain had started in late May and now, mid-August, it was still raining. But the day broke clear that Sunday morning and Earle, Tom, Roland, and I with the Remington, a .20 gauge double-barrel shot gun, and fishing tackle, piled into my mother's white four door 1951 Lincoln and headed for the ranch.

We drove ten miles, found a liquor store, and drove ten more miles to the ranch. Tom swung open the gate and we drove onto the spread. As we made our way along a dirt road to the catfish hole, we saw dozens, maybe hundreds, of decaying beef carcasses. Buzzards were feasting and the stench was unbelievable. Someone later said that the incessant rain had brought hoof and mouth disease, but I'm not sure.

Fortunately nothing had died at the shoreline where we were going to bob for catfish. We unloaded everything; tackle, sandwiches my mother had made, and the beer Earle had bought with a fake ID. But we had forgotten hooks. Tom and I got into the car and headed to the caretaker's cabin which we had passed a few miles back.

I don't remember why but I had the shotgun across my lap pointed outside, and Tom had the Remington. Tom's magazine was stuffed with eighteen long rifle .22s and I had both barrels loaded ... I thought. Thirty yards ahead, on my side, were two buzzards yanking on a decaying beef cow. I slowed the Lincoln to a crawl, and as we inched closer one of the birds took wing.

The other danced around but decided to continue feasting. I got within ten feet and moved the shotgun as slowly as I could until both barrels were right on the buzzard.

"I am going to knock down a damn buzzard!" I thought as I unleashed one of the barrels at point blank range. The tight spread of buckshot knocked the buzzard for a loop and Tom and I got out to watch the suffering bird struggle. I stepped closer to put it out of its misery, raised the shot gun and pulled the second trigger. Nothing. The metallic click of the firing pin seemed to resurrect the buzzard and he regained his footing and came at us. We spun back onto the road, Tom yelling "AHHHHHH!" and dashed away from the idling Lincoln, the buzzard on our heels.

Tom could have easily fired at the pursuer; he had enough semi-automatic firepower to finish off the mortally wounded buzzard. But at that moment, escaping the talons and snapping beak of our predator was his only thought, and the slowest guy in the history of Edison Senior High passed me like I was standing still.

Too scared to look back, we continued for a hundred yards. But the buzzard had dropped and died not too far from the Lincoln.

You cannot imagine the size of these things. We retrieved some hooks from the ranch hand and returned to the scene and got out. Tom lifted the bloody mess onto the hood of my mother's white Lincoln, positioned its head over the hood insignia, and spread its wings from fender to fender, the wingtips draped to the front tires. With our customized 1951 Lincoln we drove back to Earle and Roland at the fishing hole and frenzies of laughter.

XXVII. KEN'S HYDRO-ELECTRIC

Sometime around 1920, two rich Lake Placid, New York ski resort members stumbled across the little town of Lake Stearns, Florida. Thinking they could build a *summer* resort to replicate the millions generated by the New York site, they constructed a lakefront fifty-room hotel, tennis courts, golf course, and docks on a large lake that was three miles south of the town. They brought in power boats, fishing boats, and a few jeep-like, four-wheel drive sand buggies. They chartered the "Lake Placid Club" and took over Highlands County. They renamed the lake and the town and waited ... and waited. Mid-Florida summers are brutal. The Florida coastal breezes are non-existent and there are no deciduous to absorb the daily saunas.

Summer golf on a Florida coastline course is uncomfortable at best but golf inland is unimaginably harsh. The heat and humidity are unbelievable, and even with a shirt on you get sunburned.

The beautiful fresh water lake, water skiing, swimming, and fishing were enough to hold things together for awhile but the golfing activities soon ground to a halt.

Southern boys sometime enjoy summer golf but not the rich New Yorkers of the 1920s. Ninety-five degree days, choking humidity, no moving air, no shade trees, and no one finished eighteen holes.

Within months the fairways and greens had gone to seed, the starter's shack abandoned, and the "Lake Placid Golf Academy" was dead in the water.

A shower, dinner, drinks, and to bed. With no air-conditioning and the night's temperature still hovering at eighty five, one begins to understand why the New York crowd called it quits after two years.

The resort changed hands a number of times, including my dad and two rich dairymen brothers. I don't remember their intentions; to make money of course, but as a lake resort? A championship golf facility? A famous dining room? No one had the answer and my father took to the project as if trying to explain nuclear theory. He knew nothing about hotel and restaurant management but assumed he and the brothers would soon be rolling in mounds of cash.

The dairymen financed the deal and my father ran on-site operations. George Jr. was away at college so any free labor, *forced labor* I might add, came from Ken and me. I was fourteen, Ken seventeen, and being summer slaves to my father was the last thing either of us wanted.

I'll be honest; I got off rather easy. They soon decided I was too young to wait tables so I ran errands, played a little golf, raced the one remaining sand buggy through the palmetto forests, and frolicked in the lake.

Ken on the other hand spent the most tortuous time of his life. My father hired a wait staff and assigned Ken to the Hydro-Electric dishwashing machine. Trying to figure out how to kick things off, George Sr. decided on a Sunday afternoon dinner, something that would become popular and attract the Highlands County bluebloods. He purchased cheap advertising and flaunted "Sunday Dinner by the World Famous Chef Luis Lefebvre, The Lake Placid Resort, 2-5PM."

We had never heard of Chef Lefebvre, because he didn't exist. *Lod* was our chef. I don't remember where the name came from, only that he had done some of his cooking for the Florida Department of Corrections at Raiford.

Meal one was beyond disastrous. At first they trickled in, a couple, a small family, two couples. Perhaps fifty guests answered the advertising that day and as things backed up, my dad's glee turned to concern, concern to worry, worry to dread, dread to outright panic. The service was agonizingly slow, the cold food warm, the hot food cold, and when the initial complaints started, the upheaval built to an avalanche.

My father's self-assigned role as Maitre d' quickly changed to that of a slave of his own invention. He was waiting tables, busing, responding to complaints, sweating, barking at Ken and the wait staff, and totally bewildered.

As the afternoon heat took its toll, he removed his coat and loosened his tie. Soon, his white shirt was blotted orange, red, and brown, his tie stained beyond repair.

He resorted to reusing dirty linen and in the dishwashing room Ken could not keep up with his Hydro-Electric, a machine that came with the resort's original owners. A waiter quit one hour into the debacle, about the time the bearings in Ken's machine seized, arcing the thirty year old wiring. The burning spread a putrid stench throughout the kitchen and dining room. Diners were using our dirty linens to cover their mouths and noses when my dad ordered Ken to seal the door and hand-wash everything.

A family of four got up and left after a half hour of nothing but room temperature water. We were out of ice, clean napkins, tablecloths, and out of answers. Soon another table left, then another. No one paid for anything and suddenly, my father's kick-off, grand gala reopening of the Lake Placid Resort was a Highlands County joke.

After five hours of uninterrupted hell in a cramped, steamy, one hundred ten degree sealed dishwashing room, Ken emerged a changed man. He was exhausted, filthy, sweaty, mad as a swarm of Africanized bees, smelled like rotting meat, and itching for a fight.

I made the mistake of playfully tossing a rock at him as he walked across a grassy mound to his room. He rushed me, swinging those long arms and before I knew what had happened, I was sprawled on the ground with my left eye closing, a gash on my chin, and a knoll building on my upper lip.

XXVIII. RUN-INS

Sometimes I think I'll just stay with local umpiring where all the formal intricacies aren't so damn important. Watch me conclude a six inning Major Division game in an hour and fifteen minutes, see me manage the game, and notice my interactions with the players, coaches, and fans, and you'd think I've been doing it for years. Mac will watch the same game and call my cell phone cursing.

After I had gotten comfortable with organized umpiring I began to toy with the notion of advancing ... high school, Little League tournaments, etc. I was pounding the rules book and studying on-line baseball rules. I'm proud of what I've learned and I still want to improve, but if everyone thinks I'm too old to go any further, I'll stick with just the local stuff, use my timing, and make calls the way I want.

My diary notes the first game of the season, "3/5/09." I'm the base guy and big Vic is doing the plate. Vic is probably in his sixties and is one big man; probably six two and around 275. He's big all over; big arms, big torso, big head, big everything. He's never much liked me; he never acknowledges my presence on the field, doesn't introduce me at the plate, and won't accompany me on and off the field. Umpires accompany one another on and off the field to demonstrate solidarity, support, and unity. Vic uses his size to intimidate the new guys and ignores the etiquette of umpire breeding to keep an inexperienced guy in his place.

In the second inning he misses, or ignores, my signal for an infield fly situation. I'm in the C position and give it repeatedly. There's one out and runners on first and second. He ignores me and I'm wondering if it's deliberate. Finally, I call his name and repeat the signal.

One of two signals for this situation is acceptable; a right fist thumping the left pectoral or a right index finger touching the bill of the cap. The senior guys do the bill of the cap; the Major League umpires don't do anything. They don't need to; the rules are so engrained that reminders aren't necessary. I've been taught chest-thumping. Vic looks at me and does nothing. "Fuck you," I think.

There are a lot of umpire signals in Little League. There's a fair signal, a foul signal, a safe signal, an out signal, the infield fly rule signal, a he-left-the-base-too-early signal, a time-out signal, a timing signal, ad infinitum. I think the most common base-to-plate (or vice versa) signals are time out, infield fly, and timing.

"I'll call safes and outs on the bases but Fat Ass can do the rest of this game by himself," I thought. From the C position, the base umpire has a good angle on balls and strikes. I saw several pitches that were right on, that Vic called balls.

I had another run-in with Vic in a later game. We're at the Lehigh complex doing a Major Division game, Vic again the plate, me on the bases. I'm in the C position and there's a play at third and the throw arrives well before the runner. But again, the tag doesn't get there and as the runner slides in, the tag is *then* dropped all the way. But too late and I call "Safe!" with my arms spread.

The head coach, Felix, a Mexican guy I really like, is granted time by Vic and trots out to my position.

"Felix, I saw what you saw," I say stupidly, trying to finish this before it gets started. It's my third game of the day and neither words nor thoughts were forming with any clarity. I wanted to say that I knew what the play *looked like* but that it didn't happen the way it looked

"Good; then you'll change the call," he said, turning away.

"No."

I think he was having a little fun with me but I'm not sure. He turned back.

"But … but … if you saw it the way I saw it, why aren't you changing it?"

I was so tired that I had forgotten *what* I had seen and couldn't seem to vocalize that the tag had not been applied.

"Uh, Felix, the call stands."

"But you said you saw what I saw and I saw the tag."

"Sorry, Felix, but I'm not changing the call."

He shrugs and returns to his dugout. I am astounded as Vic waves me in. This would be the first time another umpire has questioned one of my calls and I can't believe it's happening. I am *not* going to him. If he wants to horn in on one of my judgment calls, he's coming to *me*. He walks out and confronts me menacingly, "Do you want to change the call?"

"Why should I?"

"It was a terrible call."

"He didn't get the tag down. If it was a terrible call, *you* change it."

"Are you going to change it? It was a terrible call."

The situation is more embarrassing than anything. One umpire berating another for alleged dishonesty.

He goes back to the plate and my anger slowly builds. After the third out I walk back towards the A position, seething. I was so angry that I was afraid I would ruin my concentration and I was begging myself to stay focused.

I'm a person who needs to vent, to finalize, to clarify, to find blacks and whites to everything, a trait that is wasteful, time-consuming, and harmful to myself and people around me.

Mac walks to the fence and calmly says, "Make your out calls with your right hand."

"Mac, did you just see that?"

"No," he lies.

"That son of a bitch had no right to do that. I've only been umpiring a year and he's supposed to be a senior umpire and he's a piece of shit."

Mac turned away with what I thought was a slight smile and said, "Make your out calls with your right hand."

I had vented but it wasn't over. I tried not to worry about Vic's size because I knew there would be more to come. After the game we exited the field separately and I tracked him down outside of the playing area.

"Vic, you shouldn't have done that."

"Done what?"

"Questioned my judgment; questioned a judgment call of a fellow umpire."

"Our job is to get it right," he snarls, moving a step closer.

I got in a lot of fights as a kid and I've had my nose broken, my lips lacerated, teeth chipped, eyes blackened, a rib broken, and my ears rung. I won some of the fights but usually because I knew how to pick opponents. And a lot of the fights in which I got my ass kicked were episodes of anger overwhelming rationality.

Vic was huge but I wasn't backing down, and I was too mad to let things die. I stand my ground, put a finger in his face and say too loudly, "You were wrong! You screwed up! Don't ever do that to me again; you were wrong!" Some fans spilling out of the stands paused and watched our confrontation and later, I was thankful for their intervention. Big Vic would have eaten my lunch.

More than anything, the event saddened me. Little League baseball shouldn't be this important to anyone other than the kids.

Everyone at all levels of umpiring is watching out only for his own butt. All of us think we're Big League baseball umpiring prospects and secretly, we want to move out of volunteerism to the $250,000 annual salaries of the John Hirschbecks. We want to "HOO-A" an A-Rod out on strikes and heave a steamed Lou Pinella in front of 40,000 ballistic fans. Likewise we think our umpiring contemporaries are pieces of dog doo-doo. I watch a lot of umpiring from the stands and see all kinds of mistakes, stuff that I think is downright, well, little leaguish.

I recently watched some postseason all-star Junior Division games. In the second game I saw, jealously, that Ike was doing third in a four-man. The plate guy was almost Vic's size, and wore outlandish patent leather shoes and belt. His calls seemed okay but nothing else did. He squatted behind the catcher with a humped spine and protruding groin and looked like a dog taking a crap. One called strike would be an Ike fist to the pitcher, the next a finger pointed to first base like I do. He sported a weird version of a Fu Manchu, a gray combined moustache and beard with tips of ugly hair protruding well below his face mask. **Where do they get these guys?**

I can't believe someone like *Dogchu* was chosen over me to do these games. I hope it's because Mac wants me to take time for the hip thing and not because he thinks I'm a crappy umpire. Sometimes I want to scream at him, "I want a grade! I want to know how I'm stacking up against Vic and Ike and Brett and The Kid! Give me a freekin' *F* but give me something!"

My thoughts the night of the Vic encounter, as I was writing in my diary, were to find some kind of compensatory umpiring; something that would pay you if you did a decent job or fire you if you didn't. I was floating around in a daze not knowing if I was a good umpire or a bad umpire. I suppose the truth lies somewhere in between.

No one my age is getting into professional umpiring; the numbers don't allow lots of newcomers and the politics and ass-kissing are rampant. I'm comfortably retired, my wife programs computers for the state of Florida, loves her job, makes a nice salary, and we don't need the travel, the moves, nor the $2500 annual salary. The competitive part of me, however, would like a chance at higher skilled games. And the urge to get better tugs at me constantly.

XXIX. RULES AND BALKS

The Majors Division, usually ages nine to twelve, uses the infield fly rule but not the uncaught third strike rule. The next division, the Juniors, usually twelve to fourteen, does use the uncaught third strike rule. I umpire the two divisions back and forth and it is worrisome having to invoke one rule one night and something different the next. The base-running rules differ also.

I was using a scab one night in a Juniors game and he had the entire infield responsibility. A runner rounds third, heads for home, and the throw to the plate will nail him easily. He realizes his plight and jerks to a stop halfway home and turns back. A classic rundown. The catcher fires to the third baseman and the runner turns again. The catcher has correctly moved up the line while the pitcher comes home to cover the plate.

The return throw to the catcher is true and as the runner is about to be tagged, he lurches out of the way, into the infield grass, and sprints for home. The scab had been in the C position and had moved over to make the call. "Safe," he mumbles, not sure of anything. In umpiring the closer the play, the more you have to *sell* the call. "Out!" I bellow at the same time and I'm into my first official baseball rhubarb. The offended manager sprints from his dugout yelling, "Aw c'mon, Mike!"

"Doug, he was out of the base path."

"He can leave the base path; look at the rules!"

In Little League there *are* hazy rules about the subject and about collisions between runners and defensive players, and about sliding.

I wave over the scab and ask, "Why did you call *safe?*" Not being experienced means in my mind that I *do* have to be straightforward. I want Doug to hear everything between scab and me.

"The catcher missed the tag … I thought," he gulps. I had assumed that's what he saw but wanted to make sure.

"Doug, my call stands."

"Mike, the rules say he can leave the base path."

I wasn't sure and again said, "My call stands. If you're going to protest do it before the next pitch."

I gave myself a D that night, punishment for not being positive about a rule. The next day I found the precise rule. It allows a Junior Division runner three feet to avoid a tag. I changed my grade to a B- rationalizing the runner had gone beyond the three feet in the rundown.

The Juniors can balk, the Majors cannot. I remember the first game I ever pitched in Little League. Our coach had not spent a lot of time with his pitchers on the balk rule. In fact, he hadn't spent much time with his pitchers at all. He did a lot of infield work and we had a lot of batting practice; maybe he didn't know that much about pitching and balking.

There was a teenage umpire behind the mound calling balls and strikes. It was a practice game and we're still learning the game of baseball, most of us seven or eight years old.

A runner on and I try to go into the set position and screw something up.

"That was a balk," he says but doesn't enforce the punishment of advancing the runner(s) to the next base.

I try again.

"That was a balk."

Flustered, I momentarily forget all about the set position and go into a full windup. Remembering my mistake, I hesitate, not sure what to do.

"That was a balk."

I look at our coach, Paul Graham, pleading for help. He simply rolls his eyes. I didn't know if I should keep pitching, ask for help from the umpire, or call time.

Trying again, I toe the rubber with my left shoe, ready for another full windup. But it's the wrong starting point for a set position and I step forward to start again.

"*That's* a balk too."

I'm now bouncing between embarrassment and anger and turn to the teenager. "What do you want me to do? Is *everything* a balk?"

"Everything *you're* doing is a balk," he retorts. With no help from anyone, I'm at wits end and start throwing to the catcher as hard as I can, not caring about a windup and not caring what the runners were doing. I probably balked another fifteen times. The teenager gave up and ultimately Coach Graham replaced me.

I'm still not sure of the precise balk rules and we've received no training on the subject. Basically the rule is supposed to be called if there's intent to deceive the runner. The pitcher can fake a pickoff throw to second or to third, but not to first. He can step backwards off the pitching rubber and then do anything he wants; stop, throw to a base, fake to a base, dance, or scratch his ass. If he steps off sideways or forward, he's balked. He can fake to third or second, or both, and *then* wheel and fire to first. But he can't fake to first and wheel and fire to second or third. *And* by virtue of faking a throw to second or to third, his pivot foot comes off the rubber properly (for some reason) and then he *can* fake a throw to first.

I've called a couple of balks in the Juniors but I wasn't sure what I was doing. Sometimes, we new guys want to merely assert our right to make a call other than a ball or strike or safe or out.

A balk was called by *Dogchu* and between innings I went to the fence.

"Blue, can I ask you a question?"

Umpires are not to converse with fans, especially during tournament play but he walked over.

"Hi, I'm a district eighteen umpire and … "

"What do you want?" he demands, probably pissed that I've interrupted him.

"Do you mind if I ask what happened on that balk?"

"Yeah; the pitcher jerked his hands into the set position too fast, and then he was too slow" he answers, turning away.

I return to Barb and she asks, "What did he say?"

"I have no idea," I answer.

XXX. ANDY, CHRIS, AND MORE RULES

Barb and I belong to the Vines Country Club and I have a regular, weekly game with the "Vandals" group. Everyone throws in five bucks and each member of the winning foursome goes home with twenty or thirty dollars, depending on the number of foursomes.

Everyone meets in the Men's Grill Room, eats lunch, and someone figures out the money. When I'm a winner I'll leave a tip for Andy, the head bartender. If I don't win he gets twenty percent rolled onto our monthly bill anyway.

One day my foursome won and I celebrated with four Miller Lites before going home. I wasn't scheduled to umpire for two more nights but there's a message from Mac.

"Mike, Ike's sick and I need you to do a Majors at San Carlos."

Thanks to my former father-in-law I enjoy cold beer, but do not touch the stuff on the day of a game. I'm the only possible fill-in so take a shower, shave, and set the alarm for a two-hour nap.

I'm cranky at game time and at the plate meeting between Mike and Doug say, "I'm a last-minute fill-in and I've had four beers. If you don't want me to do the game, we can reschedule. If you do, don't give me any shit." They both smile and agree and we start. I do the entire game without a scab and without a hitch and give myself an A.

I constantly worry about the rules and enforcing them correctly. The infield fly rule gave me fits in the beginning. It is, however, a rare event, especially in the Little League divisions. The rule was designed to not allow the defense to manufacture multiple outs. Let's say there are runners on first and second and the batter hits an easy pop-up to the shortstop. Without the rule he could deliberately drop the ball, pick it up and throw to third base for a force out of the second base runner (who must stay on the bag if there's a caught fly ball) then a throw to second for a force out of the runner on first. An easy double play.

For some reason the baseball rules people don't seem to think that the same thing can happen with a runner on first base only. And ... if there's the same lazy pop-up to short, he can deliberately let the ball fall untouched, pick it up and throw to second for a force out and create (because of the Infield Fly rule) a double play. The rule is in effect *only* with less than two outs and *only* if there's a force play at third base.

It all sounds overly complicated and it is.

One or no outs and runners at first and second or the bases full, and the rule is signaled so that all the umpires are aware of the possibility of an infield fly rule.

Andy is a big guy, probably around sixty who pitched for the Orioles and Brewers. He's a great guy and likes to cut me off after one Miller Lite.

"Mike, you've had enough."

"Baloney."

"Yep; you're finished. We're closing," he'll say while drawing another beer.

I enjoy talking baseball and umpiring with Andy because of his years in the big leagues. One day we were discussing the infield fly rule.

"Andy, the infield fly rule is in effect and the batter pops it up down the first base line between home and first; I call *infield fly rule if fair,* right?

"Right."

"The ball hits untouched in foul territory but spins into fair territory while still in the infield. The infield fly rule is in effect and the batter is out, right?"

"Bulllllllshit," he says.

"That's what the rules say."

"Maybe Little League rules say that. But it hit in foul territory, in the Major Leagues that's a foul ball ... period."

"OK; what about a bunt? Suppose a bunt is laid down and it hits first in foul territory but then rolls to the chalk or all the way into fair territory?"

"Foul ball."

I'm more confused than ever. I had thought I had these two rules down pat. I had never called them but thought I could if either came up in a game. Here's a former Major Leaguer telling me I *still* don't know what I'm doing. I return home, look up the rules and call Mac. Both the rulebook and Mac confirm my versions and the next day I confront Andy.

"I was right; the bunt is fair and the infield fly rule *is* in force."

"Gawwwdammit, Mike; how much money do you have?"

"Five bucks."

Andy's assistant bartender, Chris, is listening in.

"Mike, Andy's right."

"You want a piece of this?"

"Right on; easy money."

The discussion continues for a couple of weeks and the Vandals get involved and are divided but most agree with Andy and Chris. I keep forgetting to bring in the rules book but Andy wouldn't have accepted the Little League version anyway.

A few weeks later a group of club members and some of the staff attend a Fort Myers Miracles game together.

The Miracles belong to the Minnesota Twins and are in a Class A league. It is decent baseball and I enjoy watching the two-man crews. We've had several beers and Andy goes to the backstop and talks to the plate guy who he knows. He comes back to our seat and hands me a five dollar bill. Chris is several rows away and several beers ahead of us. I make my way to him, holding up Andy's five dollars with an ear-to-ear grin. Chris is around thirty, a big guy who works out. He fishes out a five dollar bill and raises his hand to high-five me. I greet him and he whacks my right hand, spraining my wrist. I won ten bucks that night but paid dearly.

A few weeks earlier, and before my run-in with Vic, I'm discussing the rule with him.

"There's no such thing as *if fair*. Who told you that? If it's foul, it's foul. No one calls, *infield fly rule if fair.*"

Some of the rules of baseball confound both players *and* umpires.

The *uncaught third strike* rule gets dicey too. Its intent is to ensure that there is complete control of the ball if an out is to be called. A batter swings and misses strike three or a third strike is called, and the ball is either dropped by the catcher or skips past. If there is no runner on first, the batter can try and reach the base before the throw beats him or he is tagged out.

The purpose of the rule, like the infield fly rule, is to not allow the defense to manufacture multiple outs. Without the rule and a runner on first, the catcher could deliberately drop the ball at his feet, pick it up and throw to second for the first out of a double play.

However, with two outs and therefore no possibility of a double play and a runner on first, the batter *can* try for first.

I'm doing the plate one night and Brett is in the B position with a runner on first, one out. The batter swings at a third strike and there's a passed ball. The batter flings his bat and wrongly starts for first. A lot of the coaches simply tell their batters to run if a third strike hits the dirt; most of them aren't sure of the rule but don't want to miss an opportunity for a base runner. I'm limping down the line behind the batter, calling, "Batter's out! Batter's out!" The runner on first pays no attention to me, and seeing the batter coming at him, breaks for second. The runner taking another base is within the rule and he trots into second. The batter finally hears me, realizes he's out and almost to first, turns and heads for his dugout. Now the runner sees the batter leave and *walks* back to first, apparently thinking that he was *not* entitled to second base. Someone puts the tag on him and Viola! a double play.

One of the challenges of umpiring, especially Little League, is that this stuff has to be called fast and it has to be called right. There's no NFL replay and sometimes there's not even a fellow umpire to ask for help.

XXXI. BASEBALL, SOFTBALL, STRIKES AND FANS

Early in the 2009 season I was getting a lot of complaints about balls and strikes. I like low stuff and if a Little League pitcher (of any division) can keep his pitches low, I want to reward him. That's how the Major Leaguers pitch; the pitchers who don't throw ninety-five miles an hour but can throw low breaking stuff are usually pretty good.

My concept of the strike zone is, correctly, that it is three-dimensional and that the white rectangle they impose on TV screens is terribly misleading because it's only two-dimensional. A ball that kicks up dirt behind the plate is always thought to be "low." But what if it enters the strike zone at the front of the plate at the knees and *then* dives into the dirt? To me, that's a strike. A ball that the catcher takes six inches inside is always a ball, "inside." But what if it had entered the three-dimensional strike zone waist-high, caught a corner of the plate and then curved to the inside? That's also a strike but it's never called.

NBC's *Game of the Week* crucifies a plate umpire for calling a strike on any pitch that's caught outside of the network's little white rectangle. Nonsense. To make the strike zone an accurate illustration, the TV producers need to superimpose some type of three-dimensional box and show where the pitch entered and where it exited. I've had a number of run-ins with coaches who don't like my strike zone. I've tried to sell the idea that it isn't necessarily where the pitch winds up but also where it *enters*. But it's a hard sell and I know there have been some complaints that have gotten back to Mac. I *have* inched up my strike zone but I never want to take away anything from a young kid who can keep his pitches down.

I also enjoy watching the breaking pitches come in. There are only a few Major Division pitchers who try to throw breaking stuff, but a lot of the Juniors have mastered the curve ball. I'll try and give a lot of the plate to a kid trying to throw a curve, slider, or cutter. The rear-back-and-fire-it-as-fast-as-you-can approach to pitching gets monotonous. Every other pitch is a passed ball, especially in the younger divisions. But a young guy trying to throw a curve ball is fun to watch and you have to determine if any part of the pitch caught the plate (or my three-dimensional strike zone). Breaking stuff keeps you on your toes and makes you concentrate.

Most of the hitters haven't learned to deal with good breaking pitches. A breaking pitch will come in, heading for the batter's noggin and he'll dive out of the way as the ball breaks over the plate. "HOO-A!" and the batter will look at me like I'm crazy.

In mid-March I did a girls' fast pitch. I'm not sure how the girls break down their divisions but I always seem to be doing Seniors. Some of the pitching is quite good and I'm always surprised how well the catchers handle the hard stuff. The *whack!* of a hard pitch into the catcher's glove is every bit as loud as a Junior's fastball.

The only thing about doing fast pitch softball is that you can't seem to make the players hustle between innings. In Little League, I'll study the pitcher warming up, the catcher who's still putting on his gear in the dugout, and determine if any of it is wasting time. If I don't think there's a deliberate attempt to hustle between innings, someone is going to pay. A coach can put a kid behind the plate to take warm up pitches if the regular catcher is still gearing up. At the plate meeting the umpires usually demand "One minute between innings; that's all you get." However the warning is seldom enforced. If no one is there to take the warm up pitches, as soon as the real catcher arrives, I order, "Throw it down; let's go!" The team has lost its right to warm up pitches and no one seems to care.

The difference between Little League and the girls' fast pitch is the difference between scowls and tears. I can ride herd on a Juniors' boy who is loafing but I can't seem to handle girls the same way. I can scream "LET'S GO!" to a Majors' team playing grab-ass when they should be taking the field but I can't do that with the girls. With the girls, I'll take Keith the San Carlos coach aside and say something like, "How 'bout it? Can you put some fire under them?" but it doesn't work; girls are girls.

I was doing a girls' game and we were an inning away from the mercy rule. Keith was leading 21-0 and his team was batting in the top of the fourth. There were no outs, the bases loaded, and the game was eternal. I called my own time and walked down to his third base box.

"Keith, c'mon; let's get this shit over. How 'bout some outs?"

"I agree," he says.

He starts walking the runner on third to the plate between pitches. The other team doesn't get it, the catcher looks at the runner walking towards her and throws the damn ball back to the pitcher! The runner steps on the plate, another run. Now Keith calls time and talks to his batter. She starts deliberately missing every pitch and strikes out. He then talks to his next batter and the same thing happens. Finally the third out and we ultimately get the game over. But some of the girls' games are competitive and when there's good pitching, their games can be fun.

I did the plate in a Majors game right after the girls' game. Mike was one of the coaches and inserted himself in the third base coach's box as most of the head coaches do. Mike's batter squares to bunt and as the pitch comes in shoulder-high, there's a slight movement of the bat.

"HOO-A!" I yell. A bunter can leave the bat over the plate if he's going to let the pitch pass and a ball out of the strike zone is still a "ball." But if he attempts to hit the pitch by moving the bat, it's a strike.

Mike breaks from the box and runs towards me. I'm into the fourth inning of my second game and once again, I'm tired and my hip hurts.

"Mike," I yell, "don't even try."

He returns to the coaching box, mumbling something I couldn't hear.

With two outs, Mike has another runner on third. The catcher goes brain dead and heads for his dugout. The pitcher has his back turned to the plate, ball in hand. There's not a soul at the plate but me. Mike's runner could have crawled home but stays glued to the bag. The catcher enters his dugout, realizes his mistake, and runs back to the plate, probably saving a run. Between innings, I intercept Mike.

"Mike," I joke, "you and your runner OK?"

"Don't start," he snarls.

Squawking about balls and strikes is supposed to be an automatic ejection. The plate umpire hears grief from the stands all the time but it's usually not said directly to his face. "Knees to the armpits, Blue; knees to the armpits." I'll usually leave it alone but for sport sometimes I'll turn and try and catch the culprit. Despite what good umpiring dictates, I try and interact with the fans. I truly enjoy walking to the fence in front of the fans of the offended team and ask, "Did I screw that up?" or "He *was* out, wasn't he?" It's surprising what some of the replies are. Seldom does anyone reply with malicious answers. I'll hear things like, "You may have gotten it, Blue." or "It was close." or "Naw; you blew it." One night a father answered, "It was the correct call, Blue; you're doing a helluva job." After the game as I'm walking to the Umpire's room, this same father corrals me and says, "We're moving and I'm taking my son out of this league. I think you should do the same thing."

I stopped and faced him, "What's *your* problem?" something I should never have done. Before he could answer or before it went any further, Tina's husband came up behind me, took a fistful of my shirt and pushed me to the door of the Umpire's room.

The next night I was doing a Juniors game and one of the teams has a 14-year old, six feet two, who could throw fire. I caught a pitch in the throat somehow and it scared the crap out of me. We (and the catchers) wear dangling throat protectors, hard plastic plates that are attached by Velcro to the bottom of the mask. The bottom edge hangs to about mid-chest. Somehow this pitch got under the throat protector and hit me in the Adam's apple. I assume it glanced off something first but since that incident, I constantly check that my throat protector is hanging correctly and not tucked someplace. I see the Major League umpires also constantly fingering their throat protectors.

It's funny (and scary) what baseballs will sometimes do once they've crossed the plate. Foul tips happen all the time of course but the ones that are tipped straight back after being thrown by a 6'-2" cannon are the worst. Sometimes I'll hear the sound of the bat tipping the ball, then the sound of the ball nicking the glove, and then the sound of the ball rocketing past my ear. It all happens in microseconds. Or the ball will be tipped into someone's shin protector and then into the plate. Bing!Bang!Zip! By the time I realize how close I've come to death, the pitcher is delivering the next fast ball.

It is good for someone my age to have to stay constantly focused. The Texas Double-A coach who was killed along the first base line in 2007 was *not*, I assure you, staying focused.

Staying focused is an extremely serious part of umpiring. I'll bend over to sweep the plate but before I do, I'll make damn sure the batter is aware of me and standing away from the plate. Some kid taking leisurely cuts at imaginary pitches could easily knock me cold. I also make sure the pitcher is aware of my being exposed. I yell, "Time!" while looking at the pitcher and throw up my hands, giving the time-out signal. I don't want some fireballer hitting me in the ass while I'm sweeping the plate.

In my Little League pitching years I often heaved pitches when the batter wasn't there, the catcher wasn't there, and the umpire was standing aside. I guess I would be thinking about anything but pitching and just rearing back and throwing. The fact that the inning had not started and that no one was at the plate did not register. Pitching for me was just trying to get the ball somewhere near the plate. There were no signals, no targets, just some obscure zone to throw a baseball through. I would gun a pitch at nothing.

The ball would hit the dirt or screen and people would look at me like I didn't have all my oars in the water. I got used to it though. When it happened, I would windmill my left arm as if trying to loosen it, hoping that they would think a pitch left my hand unintentionally.

XXXII. POST SEASON

I am three days before total left hip replacement. I hope I'm recovered by Fall Ball. I watched a Florida State Juniors Regional playoff game today. Mac had asked me to be water boy, to fetch water for the four-man crew. The thought occurred to me that I had advanced to George Jr.'s Team Manager title. It was hot, probably a heat index of around 110 degrees.

I sat in the scorer's box behind the plate, a very interesting place from which to watch a game. The pitching is better at this time of year and it's fun to watch the pitches dive in or down. The scorer's box is maybe six feet off the ground giving a good angle from higher up. Every third inning I would grab four bottles of iced water and run them to each umpire. It was steamy hot and all four of the umpires were soaked in sweat as soon as the game started. This was Juniors all-star playoffs and compared to the local version, very good baseball. One team was from the Tampa area, the other from around Orlando.

I now know why I'm not a good umpire. I'm doing okay and I'll get better but this four-man crew was outstanding. I can't rotate a three-man; God knows what'll happen with a four-man. The four umpires were flashing signals back and forth and all four participating in a moving, flowing recital of umpiring that was glorious to watch. And some of their signals were things I had never seen.

Ike's all-star experience did not go well. The night after Barb and I watched him do third, he did first base in a four-man. On a close play in the second inning some kid said "Dumb ass" and Ike immediately tossed him. Happens that this was that team's best player, their catcher.

An ejection from one game means an automatic suspension from the following game. To lose a "franchise" player for the better part of two games in double elimination format usually spells doom for the affected team. So Ike's heave-ho is a telling moment, something like the butterfly wing-fluttering that ignites global events. This kid was to have been his team's ticket to Taylor, Michigan, the site of the Junior Division World Series. The coach comes to the infield and confers with Ike. Ike explains that his player cursed, an automatic ejection. The coach explains back that nothing was directed at the umpiring, that the kid was hanging the label "Dumb Ass" on himself for making an out. The coach is desperate to get the ejection reversed but is getting nowhere with Ike. Without his .700 batting average catcher, he and the rest of his team were going nowhere. He begs Ike to reconsider the ejection then asks the other umpires to intervene. So there's a four-man conference being conducted while the team's fans are laying plans to lynch poor Ike.

Ike is a nice kid; reticent and shy. As he's relating the incident to me four days later there's no smile on his face, no humor in his voice. He seemed genuinely depressed by the event and ended the tale by saying, "I'm out of postseason; they're not going to let me do any more games."

The crew-chief listens to Ike's version, listens to the kid, listens to the manager, and asks the other two umpires what they saw or heard. He then demands that any decision is to be Ike's, that there will be no appeal to the other umpires. The opposing manager, realizing the enormity of the moment and aware that people were trying to overturn the ejection, has now joined the infield meeting. He's staring at Ike, daring him to change his call. Ike is screwed. He's probably made a bad decision but there's no way to change it. The other umpires, the player, the two coaches, and two hundred fans are looking at Ike, waiting.

"My call stands," he whispers, wanting to crawl into a hole. For the rest of the game, the verbal assaults from the seats were unending and the umpire-in-chief allowed it.

Ike made the mistake of sitting in the stands of this team's second game the next night. The anger continued and he was getting concerned for his safety and left. This team lost both Ike's game and the next one and drove home to Pensacola in a state of disbelief. One of the Juniors pre-World Series national favorites and the pre-Florida regional favorite had been done in by a questionable umpiring decision.

Maybe the reason Ike's ejection was so profoundly bad was something that happened a few night's later. A batter is called out on strikes and as he's walking to the dugout, slings his bat into the fence. Another *automatic* ejection; but as Roy is walking toward the player, the head coach sprints out of the dugout to his angry player, gets in his face, and screams, "That was the most stupid thing you could do!" Everyone heard it of course and the coach rants on and on at the poor kid who starts tearing up. Roy hesitates, not wanting to add more hurt.

"Yer gonna send us *all* home, you bonehead! Apologize to him right *now!*" He still could have been ejected but sometimes prudence takes priority over our need to be authoritative. The thrown bat was not an attempt to show up the umpire but an act of self punishment, of anger. The three huddle, the umpire doing most of the talking. The kid says something to the umpire, his head hung in utter shame. It's over and the poor kid walks to the dugout, trying to hide his tears. But he stays in the game. Mac was standing behind me at the scorer's table and says, "This is a real teaching moment; remember it."

Vic, Ike, Joe Craig, and two or three other idle District 18 umpires and I were standing around after today's game, before the start of the next game. Whenever two or more umps get together; we love to tell umpiring stories and I like to use the opportunities to also ask questions and learn. Joe was doing first on a four-man last week. It's the playoffs, two outs, two strikes, and a big homerun hitter on a Miami team lunges at a pitch, tries to hold up, and awkwardly jerks the bat to a stop. But he committed and is correctly rung up. The big kid slams his bat into home plate with a "FUCK" that was heard all over Lee County. The plate guy immediately tosses him.

The kid's father sitting in the stands along the first base line stands up and screams at his kid, "What the fuck did you do *that* for?"

The plate guy loses it, keeps his mask on, calls time and motions for Joe to come in for a make believe conference. The plate guy is bent over, one hand rubbing an imaginary sore thigh, the other pinching his nostrils. He doesn't bother to remove the father because he was leaving with his kid anyway.

XXXIII. EJECTION, HEAVE-HO, "YOU'RE GONE!"

Midway through the season I'm doing the plate. One of the teams is Tom's with his sassy outfielder son. Tom also has a catcher, a big kid whom I genuinely dislike. He baits me whenever he can, taking things to the precipice of ejection. He's good at manipulating my anger but not that good of a ball player. He bullies the smaller kids and walks around with a scowl.

One of the first things I learned was that if we can make decisions without creating scenes, without controversy, and without confrontation, it is the preferred method. Despite my flashes of anger, I've tried to practice this notion but throughout the season I've given this catcher too much leash.

He's at bat, takes a called strike, and steps out of the box to rewrap his Velcro batting gloves a la the Derek Jeters of Major League baseball. He steps into the box and holds his rear hand up to me, signaling that's he's not ready. He steps out again, taps the bat against each shoe, and reenters holding up his hand.

"Let's go, Nat."

There's a very precise rule in the book that addresses a batter deliberately delaying the game ... just start calling strikes. He steps out again.

"HOO-A!" I yell too loudly, remembering the rule.

Nat looks at me, mouth open. One word and he would have been tossed but he says nothing and thinking it was the third strike, heads for his dugout. Halfway there, I scream "HOO-A!" again and make my called third strike signal, each balled fist throwing an imaginary punch. Tom explodes from the dugout.

"What was *that* about?"

"Tom, he was delaying the game. The rules say to start calling strikes and I did."

"Well, why don't you just throw me out, then we can forfeit."

"Do you *want* to forfeit, Tom?" I'm perfectly willing to scrawl FORFEIT across the scorer's page and go home.

He doesn't answer and returns steaming to his dugout and we resume the game.

A few games later and again the plate with one of Tom's games and his two brats. Nat rounds third and heads for home. The catcher doesn't have a play and steps out of the way. Nat nevertheless hook-slides home trying to upend him. I go to Tom.

"That was unsportsmanlike conduct and this is my first warning. The next one and he goes!"

Tom merely nods. Tom has protected this brat from the beginning of the season and I think Tom is so removed from the unspoken declarations of baseball and sportsmanship that he should be banned. But I guess they need coaches so he still has a team.

A couple of innings later Nat comes to the plate and starts his delay antics again. He's in and out of the box, bat-tapping his shoes, and holding up his rear hand.

"Nat, get in the box and get ready or you're gone." By this time the Latino pitcher is fuming. Nat steps in, holds up his hand one more time and finally gets ready. The Latino kid fires a fastball, right on target ... and right at Nat. The big brat tries to spin away and is whacked between the shoulder blades. Nat arches his back, grimaces to heaven, howls and turns toward first, bat in hand.

At the moment I honestly did not think the pitcher did anything intentional, but his teammates converge, pounding him on the back. Half way to the base Nat slams the bat into the dirt. I race towards Tom pointing skyward with my right index finger and yell, "He's gone!"

My first ejection and it felt damn good. Tom is livid.

"Throw me out, too!" he yells.

"Nip this in the bud," I'm thinking so I turn towards the scorer's box to confirm Nat's ejection.

A Little League ejection is a big pain. Reports have to be filed, emails exchanged, and sometimes there's a hearing where both versions are dissected.

The concession stand manager is the wife of Tom and mother of the outfielder. This night, she happens to be keeping score and says, "You've got this all messed up. You don't know what you're doing."

"Lyn, that's unfair," I shoot back. "Tell you what … if you don't want me to do Juniors' games, get me suspended. But you shouldn't be involved in a game your husband is coaching and in which your son is playing."

"OK, after this game, you're suspended from umpiring and I won't do the scorekeeping anymore."

Remember, Lyn runs cheeseburgers out of the concession stand, her *only* duty, and she is suspending *me* from umpiring? I'm not sure where this is going but I *do* know Mac is going to be pissed.

After the game, the ejected kid's mother confronts me.

"What did my son do?"

"Unsportsmanlike conduct, ma'am."

"Why?"

"*Why?* What do you mean?"

"I mean what did he do?"

Exasperated, I answer, "He wasn't behaving correctly, ma'am."

"What did he do?"

"The rules say that a player can be …"

"My husband is so mad, he wants to fight."

"Where is your husband?"

"Over there; he's still in the stands."

At this point I'm really not mad at the mother but I am boiling about Lyn's *suspension*. I step around mom and head for the stands. I don't want to fight the guy but I *do* want him to know that I'll no longer kowtow to his son's bullying and antics. Halfway there, two fellow umpires intercept me and demand that I get in my car and go home.

"No fighting between a plate umpire and a player's father," one of them jokes. Some joke.

I've never heard of an ejection being reversed but it's an important decision (if it goes that far) because of the ensuing one game suspension. Usually the matter cools, the suspension is served, and everyone forgets it.

The rules say the suspended player may not enter the Little League complex until he is eligible for play. Two nights later I'm conversing with a couple of fellow umpires. We're not doing games, just watching. Nat walks by in violation of the do-not-enter rule. I want to corral him but Kevin, a very senior and very good umpire, tells me to let it go. And I do.

I was right about Mac; he *was* pissed. The district's head umpire has to get a written report from the umpire in question, that report then has to be submitted with the head umpire's report to district headquarters, the district's board of directors then decide if a hearing is justified, and it can go on ad nauseam. I send my report to Mac via e-mail and he calls my cell phone,

"Cut out all the bullshit. Do your report again, eliminate 95% of it and just tell me, in a sentence or two, what happened."

I redo everything and wait. A day later I'm told by the District 18 president, Keith, that my next scheduled game with

Tom's team was changed; instead I would be doing a girls' softball game.

"Keith, that is **not** going to happen."

"Why not?" he asks.

"Because the kid I threw out deserved to be thrown out. He's been baiting me all year, he's mean and mean-spirited, and he bullies every kid who's smaller than he is. If you do this to me, he will have won, his ways will have been vindicated, and you will have degraded my umpiring."

Keith knew I was right but I was nevertheless taken off the game, but I did not do the girls' softball. I thought my integrity was at stake and that my future umpiring was in question. I have to find "endings" to everything, and the Nat thing was no exception.

XXXIV. FATHER-SON UMPIRING

Stephen and his family visit in April. Shelley, my daughter and grandson Donovan are here also; it's a houseful. I'm anxious for everyone to watch me umpire and there's a Major Division game and I've got the plate by myself. Plans are made for the seven family members to be in the stands but Shelley, Donovan, Suzanne, and Sarah beg out so Stephen, Michael, and I drive to the ball park. Barb gets to the park ten minutes before game time.

The fun of having my whole family watch me do something I enjoy so much and their subsequent disinterest has me in a funk. No one cares squat about my umpiring, maybe as it should be. My son's world and Michael's world revolve around *Michael's* baseball. *Pops* is just an old guy with nothing left to contribute; "Let's jump in the pool!"

I ask Stephen to do the bases and we go over a couple of rotations, coverages, and review a few mechanics. He's OK with everything but says, "I'm stressed."

I conduct the plate meeting and do not reveal he is my son. In our house after the game he's describing the plate meeting.

"Pops is holding this formal *summit* and I'm like 'what's going on?' In Albany, we don't do this stuff; the umpire just says 'play ball' and we go. Pop's demanding formal answers to, 'do

116

your players understand, and play by, the rules of Little League baseball and are your players properly equipped to play according to the rules of Little League baseball?'" Stephen is doing the scene with the haughtiness of a British emissary and Michael is howling. Inside, I'm disappointed that my family is so aloof to the things I've tried to accomplish in umpiring.

The bums I've seen in Albany wouldn't be allowed to do our Tee Ball.

We decide that Barb will serve as official scorekeeper and Michael will do the scoreboard. It is Barb's first game doing the books but I'm not worried because she loves baseball and knows the rules.

A *timing* play requires the umpires to determine if a run crosses the plate before the last out of an inning. Let's say there are runners on first and third with one out and a fly ball is hit. The ball is caught for the second out. The runners tag and there's a play at second and the third out is called. If the runner from third crosses the plate *before* the out is called at second, the run counts; the run does not count if it's a fraction after the out at second.

Stephen and I screw up a timing play because he does not make *any* call on a play at second. I take off my mask and look at him while raising my shoulders with my arms out and my palms up. *Nothing*. A no-call is the worst thing that can happen. It's happened to me twice; this time with son Stephen, and another time when a scab couldn't make a decision. A no-call stops the game flow, creates confusion, and what if the runners are going non-stop? A no-call means that on-field situations have to be rebuilt, runners replaced, outs recalculated, and that someone is going to get screwed.

I've forgotten what happened with the runner on third and walk to the scene at second.

"What's the call?" I ask.

"I'm not sure; I think he went out of the base path."

"Make a call," I demand.

"I'm not sure of the rule."

"Show me how far he went outside."

"To here."

"OUT!" I yell and went back to the plate. (Remember, you have to *create* outs.) I'm ready to take a break between innings when someone in the stands asks, "Blue, does the run count?"

I had no idea; I had forgotten all about the timing play and go to Barb.

Barb has never done one of my games before but she's very bright, lettered in four sports, and was Baltimore all-county as a third baseman in high school fast pitch and, as I said, she knows baseball and baseball rules.

"Run counts," she announces.

"Run counts," I repeat and the other fans turn mean. A woman doing her own scorebook in the stands shrieks, "The run does NOT count! You're blind!" I turn away but she's on the attack.

"Ump, that's the screwiest call I've ever seen; you need another line of work, you piece of crap!"

Tina heard this one and goes to the fence at the edge of the stands and says to the lady, "One more word out of you and you're in the parking lot." The lady shuts up and I was glad someone was there to bail me out.

The rest of the game went okay but my umpiring impressed no one but myself. I need to keep reminding myself that I'm secondary when it comes to my family's baseball interests. As it should be. My fondest hope is that Michael will continue to improve and play organized baseball into his college years.

Not too long ago someone very close to me said, "Don't be concerned what others think of you and the things you do. Your concern should only be what *you* and your higher power thinks."

She's very right, of course. I love Stephen and his family very much and the fact that my umpiring means so little is becoming more okay over time.

XXXV. BUBBA

I'm not very good at the administrative part of umpiring. Rules relating to the mercy rule, time limits, maximum innings, substitutions, pitch count, etc. are things about umpiring that I can't fit into my already over-stressed brain. At every game I hope that the scorekeeper is maintaining all this stuff.

The plate guy keeps one copy of the lineup and a small notebook and pen or pencil in his shirt pocket or in his ball pouch. If there's a substitution, the coach asks for time and approaches the plate ump with the change. I'm supposed to mark it on my copy, inform the other coach of the change, and then inform the scorekeeper. The reason I'm supposed to be keeping tabs is because someone has to track the ins and outs of legal substitution. One division can switch a pitcher and third baseman and then after other described events, switch them back. Another division can't reinsert a pitcher. The subs must play a full inning and have one-at-bat before being re-substituted. I'm worried to death about balls and strikes and safes and outs and to track the rest of it becomes overwhelming.

I fake stuff a lot. A coach will call for time and say, "Eighteen for seven." I sometimes have no idea what he's talking about and a lot of times I don't hear the numbers distinctly. I'll go to the scorer's box to at least make sure *someone's* aware of what's going on and normally get waved off before I get there. District 18 has good scorekeepers who stay on top of things. Then I'll stop and pull out the lineup and pencil and pretend to be writing. What I'm supposed to be writing, I don't know.

A visiting team from Fort Myers Beach one Juniors' game. I have the plate with a scab on the bases. The scab badly blows a call and the coach comes out of his dugout.

"Coach, I'm not going to change a judgment call."

"Can I ask him for your verification?"

"You can ask me to ask him."

"OK, will you?" I normally wouldn't but both the scab and I knew he blew it, so we have a pow-wow.

Meantime, Bubba the coach's assistant has come onto the field. He's tall, ugly, mean-looking and has a goatee. I should have run him back to his dugout but didn't. You can't let the *whole* team participate in a dispute.

"The play stands," I announce.

"You're both crazy," Bubba announces to the stands.

I walk him to his dugout pulling out my little notebook and pencil. I show him a blank page, pointing to nothing with the pencil. I don't want to show him up and I don't want a scene. I want it to look like we're discussing something about a lineup.

"Bubba, it was a judgment call. The guy is not a real umpire, just a kid's father I pulled from the stands. How 'bout cutting us some slack?"

"Wellll, OK, but it was bad call."

"I know it was but if I reversed it, I'd be degrading him in front of everyone and I don't want to do that. Don't call us names anymore. I don't want to toss you. Thanks, Bubba."

He later brings us bottled water and after the game he congratulates me and shakes my hand. It probably helped that his team won.

XXXVI. GOOD MEMORIES

The good catchers make games go a lot better. They block pitches and there's not nearly as much of the back-and-forth-to-the-screen to retrieve passed balls.

Except for Nat I've built camaraderie with the catchers of both the Majors and the Juniors; it's good umpiring.

One night I was doing a Majors game and the LaBelle team had a little guy, not much bigger than Fred's boy. He was an outstanding catcher; a little pudgy but quick as a cat and he stopped everything. In between bats of the last inning, I went to his dugout and asked his coach if I could speak to his player. The little guy came out wide-eyed, thinking he had committed a baseball travesty.

"I know your team is losing but I want you to know how good you are. Nothing's gotten past you tonight. To me, you're an all-star."

I know he was proud because he was still wide-eyed when he went back to his dugout.

Perhaps my most satisfying moments of Little League umpiring are the occasions when someone stops me after a game to say, "Thanks Blue."

XXXVII. THRs AND WORLD CLASS SURGEONS

Total left hip replacement or "THR" as the surgical world calls it. I'm scheduled tomorrow at 1:00pm and so far there's been no dread, not even fright. Maybe tomorrow morning I'll wake up so scared that I won't go through with it.

Barb is taking me to a fancy steak house tonight. Is she thinking it's my Last Supper?

This morning I drove to Bonita and watched the Florida Juniors' World Series Sectional championship game. I was surprised to see Roy Toms behind the plate. He has the same experience I do and I think he's going to be an outstanding umpire. He's a genuinely nice person and he did a great job. It's so easy to critique fellow umpires while sitting in the stands. I'm sure I get the return favors. *Perrine's worthless and he's too old; let's keep him right where he is until he either quits or dies.*

One of the catchers began to complain about Roy's balls and strikes. You have to let some of that go but you also have to decide when to stop it. Roy threw up his hands, called time, and began sweeping a perfectly clean plate. I had no clue and Mac, standing next to me, again said, "Another teaching moment." While fake sweeping Roy apparently said something like, "Catch, knock it off; I'll do the umpiring." No one heard it but the catcher; no put-down, no scene, no confrontation; just a gentle reminder that the catcher was going too far.

And I got some bad news today. Tina announces that I can start umpiring again in the spring. The *spring?!!* The *spring* is five months away!

I'm all over her but she's insistent.

"We will *not* take any chances on you re-injuring your hip."

"But Tina, what if I get a clearance to umpire from my surgeon? He's telling me I can play golf in eight weeks!"

"I'll consider it but if your doctor gives you clearance to umpire by Fall Ball, your doctor's an idiot."

Maybe THR is more serious than I thought.

The overall THR experience went well. I am now fourteen days removed from the day of surgery, three in the hospital and eleven in an in-patient therapy center.

I do not remember much about the few minutes of surgery pre-op. They said something about a spinal tap, how it would be administered, what I would feel, what affect it would have. I was alarmed when the anesthesiologist told me that, during surgery, they would try and wake me up to determine if the *other* anesthesia needed strengthening. In other words, the spinal tap takes out everything from my waist to my toes and the other stuff takes out the rest of me.

"My god; I'm going to be awake when they're sawing off half of my femur?" I asked.

He assured me I wouldn't feel anything but I was still worried when they put the plastic mask over my mouth and nose.

I remember waking up with Barb trying to soothe me, whispering and rubbing my forehead. I knew they had inserted a couple of catheters; one to make sure the trachea remained open, the other a urinal catheter. The first thing I did upon awakening was to feel the end of my penis. The catheter was still there.

A week before surgery, talking to this same anesthesiologist, I had demanded, "I want my ass asleep when it goes in and when it comes out."

"You'll be asleep when it goes in and groggy when it comes out; no pain, just a *different* feeling."

A nurse came in the room and while Barb turned her head, the RN pulled down the top sheet and yanked out the tube while I screeched.

Within half an hour I started building gas and as the flatulence intensified, Barb said, "Hon, I'll be right back," and quickly left the room.

A nurse appeared with a walker and got me up and onto the walker and directed me to the toilet, shuffling behind and steadying me. The releases seemed to be timed to each agonizing step and I apologized with each fart. I later wrote notes of some of my THR experiences and of this incident they read:

"Shuffle, fart, apologize, 'it's OK, Mike;' shuffle, fart, apologize, 'it's OK, Mike;' shuffle fart, apologize, 'it's OK Mike; here you are Mike. Pull this chain when you're finished. I've got to go.'" I didn't want to be there either.

James Guerra is probably one of the world's finest orthopedic surgeons. I flipped a Harley five years ago and the Road King and I did a cartwheel. I landed on my left shoulder and the injury was severe; a total mess with massive soft tissue damage and bone displacements throughout. One of the ER doctors looked at my x-rays and predicted that all future left arm activity would be severely limited, that I would never play golf again, never throw a ball again, and that I would have to learn how to do a lot of things right handed.

A couple of months later Dr. Guerra did two very extensive arthroscopic procedures and seven months later I could shoot my usual ninety-five, throw a baseball at half speed, and had regained ninety percent mobility.

He is at the forefront of orthopedic surgery research and has invented and designed prosthetic joints, prosthetic instruments, and new techniques. To add to his busy schedule, he is often asked to do lecture series and just returned from two weeks in Osaka, Japan. He lectured and demonstrated in front of a group of international sports medicine specialists. Additionally, some of his actual procedures are televised live to foreign teaching centers.

In one of our pre-op appointments he asked if I wanted a description of the THR procedure but I had already researched it on the Internet and watched a video of the surgery. They open you up from your buttock to your thigh, cauterize the oozing blood, cut through fat, and spread the strands of muscle to expose the ball-and-socket hip joint. The top of the femur curves inward toward the pelvic bone and just above this bend at the very top of the femur is the "ball" part of the joint; the ball fits into a socket in the Ileana bone at the bottom of the pelvis.

Arthritis lays siege to the area and over time, bone spurs erupt around the edge of the joint. The surgeon shaves off the bone spurs and then saws off a couple of inches of the top of the femur, removing the bone above the bend including the ball. He then cleans out the now-empty socket and glues in a synthetic half-circle polyethylene liner. He drills a hole ten inches deep into the remaining femur and taps in the titanium prosthesis which includes the new chrome cobalt ball at the top and an eight inch spike at the bottom. The spike has a rough, textured surface that promotes bone growth and secures the prosthesis into the top of the remaining femur. The new ball is reinserted into the new socket and Viola! a THR.

North Collier Hospital is a wonderful facility, a great staff, well-organized, with the latest technology. When all the snowbirds descend on southwest Florida from December through March, NCH becomes a joint replacement Mecca. Dr. Guerra does up to six replacements a day, two days a week. And the yellow pages list a million other orthopedic surgeons.

Dr. Guerra is also the consulting team physician for the Florida Gulf Coast University sports program, the Baltimore Orioles grapefruit league, and the National Hockey League Florida Panthers. The walls of his waiting room are plastered with autographed pictures of famous athletes. Bo Jackson and

Michael Jordan are among Dr. Guerra's list of patients. Maybe it's understandable that trepidation had no part in my pre-op THR.

My eleven days of rehabbing in Estero Life Center were mostly uneventful. Institutional food that wasn't bad, and hit and miss therapy.

No wonder Medicare is going broke. For the first seven days I did not have a roommate. Three meals a day in bed, free ice cream in the afternoon, a color TV for each and every patient, wall-to-wall carpeting throughout, free daily newspapers, and a staff at my beck and call.

Mostly resort-like living and fifty percent of it superfluous. Down-in-the-dirt, grind it out therapy was perhaps all of five hours for the entire eleven days.

A good staff and they mean well. I don't know what it's like when joint replacement goes full-tilt but of perhaps twenty patients per therapy session, there were only two or three joint replacement cases. The rest of it is end-of-the-line, quivering lips, chin on chest Q-tippers who exist in a stupor and care nothing about weight-lifting or knee-bending. At first it was disconcerting to witness their suffering; then it became sad, and then it became a revelation.

My "therapy" was pedaling a stationary bike very slowly, curls and presses of a four-pound bar, balance exercises whereby a therapist and I tapped a balloon back and forth, and finally leg exercises designed to get my muscles working again. My therapist would put me on one-half of a king-sized mat and manipulate my legs.

One day she got me down and left for a few minutes. Another therapist put an eighty-five year old lady next to me. We had spoken earlier and I thought she was very alert despite her broken hip.

"As long as we're going to bed each other, we might as well know each other's names," I said.

"Greta," she said, laughing. Over the next couple of sessions, Greta and I became good buds.

In the morning sessions I would go into the PT room and hand out copies of lyrics of popular tunes. I'd then lead the group in song. Barb would find a particular song on the Internet that someone had requested, print it, make ten copies, and bring them in at night. I'd hand out the copies in the morning and everyone seemed to enjoy starting the day with music. I sing as well as I play golf, but no one cared. When I got requests for "Has Anyone Seen My Gal?" and "Chatanooga Choo-Choo", I thought it was time to let someone else do the morning music.

Keith and I became roommates on day seven. He was tall, gangly, in his eighties and had suffered a stroke, broken a hip, and was in advanced dementia.

Poor Keith would cry in agony as the nurses tried to get him into bed. His cries were painful to listen to. They would draw a curtain between our beds so I couldn't see what was happening and I would plug my good ear, trying not to hear. One night after a particular extended groaning session, his sounds morphed into melody. Barb was with me and we were trying to watch television. I began to harmonize with Keith, and Barb begged me to stop while Keith's nurses cracked up. I hope it's OK to find humor in another's suffering.

Later Barb rose to leave and I got into my walker. I walked her to the front entrance each night. As we passed Keith I said, "Hang in there, Bud." He replied only with the glassy eyes of someone who had been clubbed.

That night Keith's nurses were trying to get him to take a pill but he was fighting tooth and nail.

"Keith, open yo' mouf!" the black nurse demanded.

There was also a Latino nurse and a white nurse, two of them trying to pry down a pair of flailing limbs while the third struggled with pill insertion.

"Keith, O-PIN yo' mouf!"

He was kicking like a mule, swinging at imaginary demons and buttoned like a Zip-Loc.

"Keith, STOP it!" someone yelled, "open up!"

I was trying not to listen but realized that the white nurse and the black nurse had walked out. The remaining nurse was going to need a crow bar to open up Keith.

"Bastardo!" she hissed and walked out also.

They couldn't pay me enough to do that kind of work.

My morning songfests really helped no one. One song and it was back to whatever torture had been designated for each of the day's patients.

As the days passed, I began to formulate personal answers to the eternal questions, *When is it over? What is the end? How do I manage the diminishing time? When do I call it quits?*

At sixty-eight I was the child in the group so it was easy to put myself above the anguish that permeated our therapy sessions. My eleven day residency at a facility of people who were either dying or desperately holding to life, a hospice of Alzheimer's victims, irreparable broken hips, and folks with stroke-induced brain damage was a look into the future of physical or mental depravation. To me, it was a rehearsal of my end-of-life existence. Do I want to live a lie during my ending days? No, because when you can't umpire, can't play golf, can't ride a motorcycle, can't tell your loved ones what they mean to you, and can't be creative, it is time.

Arthritis had ravaged the spine of an old lady and she was hunched horribly. "Helen, try and sit up, dear. You're stooped over." But Helen couldn't sit up and it struck me as almost evil that her therapist could be so stupid. It was like asking a blind person to call balls and strikes.

The Pirana Club comic strip is mostly silly, in my opinion. Bud Grace isn't always funny or original but every once in a while he gets it right. One of his characters is Mother Packer, the mother-in-law of the chain-smoking Dr. Enos Pork. Mother Packer beats the crap out of everyone, including Enos. Cross her and she'll attack like a pit bull. The next panel will show Enos with black eyes and missing teeth.

We had a "Mother Packer" in therapy. I was shocked at the resemblance between a real person and an inked cartoon drawing. None of the therapists wanted to deal with her and they didn't. She was one hundred six years old, scowled at everything, and wouldn't sing my songs. I never found out why she was in therapy.

My dilemma is that, while I now had answers, both the questions *and* answers required consciousness and rationality. At certain stages of dementia, you lose interpretive reasoning. If I can survive to the exact moment, the question will be, *are you any longer creative?* If the answer is no, then my plans are to start the engine of my car parked in a closed garage. Painless, bloodless, easy; an endless sleep.

In my mind, everyone is creative. Creativity is one of the nourishments of life. Even the mindless acts of Hitler were somewhat driven by creativity.

It will be the perfect ending if after the *no* answer I can write letters to Barb and to my children, thank them for my life with them, and tell them in as simplistic language as possible how much I love them. Poof! It's over. Hell, in two generations no one will remember squat about some Little League umpire who had trouble with the strike zone.

XXXVIII. ME AND GENERAL PATTON

The plate umpire in Little League controls *everything*. Before the first pitch I have a dry mouth and butterflies but after a couple of pitches, I usually get a rush. My total command reminds me of George C. Scott in the movie *Patton*. He looks over the plains of El-Alamein while reincarnating to Hannibal before the epic Carthaginian battle against the Romans at Cannae. It was a poignant movie scene, one I'll never forget. I don't have one hundred thousand armed troops behind me but what's in front of me is *mine.*

I rule everything, the players in the field, the batter, the coaches, the dugouts, even the fans. I love the challenge of controlling everything and maintaining the ebb and flow of a well-called game. If the plate guy does his job, if positioning is good on *every* play, and if every call is made decisively and quickly, then the fans are normally appreciative of Little League umpires.

A silent appreciation seems to roll in like a fog bank, usually around the second inning; it's as though the people in the stands have overcome their initial dislike of you and they begin an understanding of the job you're doing. It's like an unspoken friendship between the fans and me.

If there's a real close play, no one knows for sure what the truth is. There will always be groans of disagreement of course but you begin to understand the meanings of the sounds coming from the stands. Certain sounds tell you that while some didn't like your call, they aren't sure themselves, and you're still OK with them. Near silence is the best sound … it means *everyone* agrees with your call. Most plays unfold easily and clearly; the silent ones. And most of the "OK"s are the close plays that you probably got right.

But have your back turned, be out of position, or make a bad rule interpretation, and the Four Horsemen are galloping towards you, weapons at the ready.

If there's a play at third and I'm by myself, I'll hustle to the bag, and while tuning my timing antenna, I'll actually be thinking about my call antics. Highly creative call antics can do a lot to overcome opposing "reads" by the fans.

"Safe!" I'll bellow, and assuming it looks like the throw beat the runner, I'll bellow even louder, "No tag! No tag!"

So far, Mac has emphasized mechanics over accuracy. And while I try to stay within his mechanics "window," I might create a dance step or two to go along with an emphatic out call.

Stand at a close play and quietly call "Out" without anything other than a raised thumb and one half of the crowd is going to be all over you.

On a close safe call, I'll squat with my arms spread and stay squatted longer than is needed. The prolonged squat says, *I got it right and don't even bother.* Do it right and despite a few groans, no one has a beef.

XXXIX. LITTLE LEAGUE WORLD SERIES

In rehab Barb came every night and stayed with me throughout both Saturdays and Sundays. We watched the TV regional playoffs of the Little League World Series.

The game between Washington and Oregon featured three of the worst calls I've ever seen. A six-man crew and a plate guy calling strikes that were a foot outside.

Where do they get these guys?

I agree that you *look* for strikes; in fact we're taught that it has to be *proven* to the plate guy that it's a ball. No proof, or in doubt, or didn't see it … it's a strike. Strike *design* is a big part of early-season baseball but in postseason tournaments and certainly World Series stuff, balls and strikes should be accurate.

The World Series plate guy seemed like he was out to prove something … like totalitarianism. *I've been selected to do the plate in a World Series game; I'm great and screw these little pricks. Cross me and I'll toss your ass.* It became a game of World Series umpire glorification and the little kids in the field played second fiddle. It's like no one grades the *Blues*. Do the same guys get selected year after year? I don't know but I *do* know ass-kissing is rampart in all levels of umpiring.

A runner on first and second, one out and the batter hits a sinking fly ball to center field. The center fielder races in, gets the ball in his glove, cocks to throw, hesitates, and finally hurtles the ball to first base to double up the retreating runner.

One problem however; the ball was trapped and not caught. Both runners see the trap and take off. The runner on second breaks for third, sees the fielder cock his arm and, confused, scampers back to second. The fielder's hesitation was that his first inclination was to get the runner at second but seeing him retreat, he threw to first because *that* runner had almost gotten to second base.

At the crack of the bat, the first base runner had correctly gone about half way to second, the proper distance to determine whether to continue advancing or to return to first in the event of a catch.

I have no idea what the rotation should have been but television showed an umpire running in from somewhere along the third base line. That umpire made the incorrect call. The second base umpire stayed glued to that bag anticipating a play. I don't know what the third base umpire did; maybe nothing. Maybe he was the Crisco Kid's buddy and taking a siesta.

There were two other bad calls but this was an inning-ending double play and had a profound effect on the outcome of the game. A six-man crew and *no* one gets it right.

For some strange reason, the plate guy signals a conference *after* the teams exchange the field and creates a cluster fuck with no end. Change the call and reverse the players? Where would the runners have ended up? How many bases was each runner entitled to? Did anyone score? Pull the kids in the dugout back onto the field and chase the kids on the field back to their dugout? The wronged coach joins the conference and politely stands aside. It's hard to believe that out of six umpires, *no* one saw the correct play. I suspect that someone *did* know the truth but reversing the exchange of the field would have been chaotic.

It was the worst call I've ever seen or heard. One side of me wants to forgive. After all, we're all amateurs and bad calls are part of our umpiring rights; but part of me wants to crucify the plate guy for not holding up the exchange of the field until *after* the conference.

At least *try* to get it right so some eleven year old kid doesn't live forever with the erroneous notion that he cost his team a World Series title.

The call stands and the coach returns to his dugout stunned and in disbelief.

It's one of Little League's problems. Ozzie Guillen or Lou Pinella would have gone ballistic but a cross word to an umpire in Little League is an ejection and subsequent one-game suspension. Little League officials have removed one of baseball's most entertaining scenes. Little League coaches always have to acquiesce; you cannot argue, you cannot curse, you cannot demand verification. As an adult I'll take the beating: reverse the call, just get it right. But don't blame a little kid for something he didn't do.

An inning later there's a hit towards first. The ball hits in the infield, in fair territory, crosses directly over the base, and settles in foul territory.

"Foul!" screams the black first base umpire and raises both hands in the air.

"A great call; Craig Clueless has made a number of great calls tonight," claims the television play-by-play announcer, Orel Hershiser, a former Los Angeles Dodgers pitcher. No one there apparently knew the rules of baseball.

The difference between a judgment call and a rules interpretation lies mainly in the notion that a rules *mis*interpretation can be appealed; a judgment call cannot. Everything favors the Little League umpire however, and even though Craig Clueless didn't know the rule he could still claim that the ball did NOT pass over the base and change his stupidity into a judgment call.

I love umpiring but Little League disagreements are almost non-existent. Wrong calls are part of the game but because the disagreements are so tame, the drama is lost. I think it's OK to say my *out* was a jackass call; just don't call *me* a jackass.

In a later inning a batted ball nicks the runner who has just left second. The ball deflects to the outfield, the runner claims third and the batter is safe at first. The rules say the runner is out at second and if there was intent, the batter can also be called out. Both runners eventually score and the game has become a distorted morass of umpiring ineptness.

What really bothered me was that, even with all his hideous errors, the plate guy was still strutting around like a peacock, as if his poor calls, his poor balls and strikes, his poor decisions, and his poor game management had all been conduct bordering on perfection. Without the threat of on-field controversy, Little League umpires aren't under any perceived pressure to get it right.

I know a lot of our district's senior guys are outstanding umpires; they've been through their reality checks, understand the umpiring hierarchy, realize they're not making the Major Leagues, but simply love what they're doing. These are the guys who conduct Mac's clinics, stay on top of the rules, and call good games night after night.

The bad umpires and the so-so umpires are the ones who should be helping some of the "coaches" in the concession stand. They provoke controversy, don't know the rules, don't know the strike zone, and assume an air of preeminence.

I remember one of Mac's clinics last year. He held it right after the World Series championship game and some of our senior umps were discussing the plate guy. Had that person been in our room, he would have been shamed out of umpiring.

XL. GOLF, UMPIRING AND RECOVERY

I sweat like crazy. South Florida summer golf gets torturous. A lot of guys in my club play as early in the morning as possible. The best tee times are before eight because by 11am, humidity blankets everything and the heat index has soared to 110 degrees. Sometimes, if you can get out early enough, you can finish a round before the dangerous part of the day begins. I start pre-hydrating the night before, wear a brimmed hat and sunglasses, slather on suntan lotion, and park the golf cart in shade every place I can.

I'll tee off at 7:45 and get to the range at seven. A couple of big cups of ice water, check in at the pro shop, some short game practice, a little putting, and then I pull out my "cannon," a driver with a head as big as a basketball. It has a very whippy shaft and I can blast balls with it about 190.

I stay on top of golf club technology; every year the guys in the pro shop sell me the latest driver, a $450 monster that "guarantees" thirty more yards.

Anyway, by the time we're on the first tee, I am soaking wet. George Jr. is a neurologist and over the years has defined every medical ailment every member of our family ever had. He once suggested my sweating could be an albino DNA trait. I'm not sure what that means.

A hot early June night and I'm doing a one-man Juniors game. The Little League umpiring uniform is hideous but it copies that of the Major League umpires. So-called plate pants have very large legs to accommodate the shin guards. Every time we're called upon to do a game, Mac demands we be prepared to do either plate or bases. To me, that means that I have to wear the very ugly plate pants to every game and if I end up doing the bases, I look like a two-legged elephant.

The pants are medium grey and turn almost black where the sweat forms. My initial sweat pours from my buttocks, then my back, then the rest. Even my sweat sweats and by the time the game starts, I am drenched. No comments yet from fans seated directly behind me, but seeing a little stubby guy, bent over the plate, with two-tone pants and a drenched, black posterior has *got* to be inviting.

In the middle of April I did the plate with Kevin on the bases. Kevin has a kid in organized baseball and umpires mostly in LaBelle. He's been umpiring for years and is one of the district's best. I asked him before the game to critique everything I did.

"The first thing I want you to do is stop moving over when the catcher moves over. Stay in your slot and it will allow you to maintain your strike zone reference." When catchers want a pitch either inside or outside sometimes they'll move six to eight inches; not just the mitt but their entire bodies. I had not heard this before and his suggestion cost me. One of the catchers moved a *lot*. If he wanted an outside corner pitch, he'd slide over maybe a foot. Now my so-called slot was alarmingly open and I felt naked. I had been taught to use the catcher for protection and Kevin was removing a lot of this protection.

My diary for that night documents eight different shots; two to the chest, one to my throat guard, two to my mask, two off my shoes, and one fast ball that plugged my left arm, dislodging the indicator. After the last out, Kevin was mostly positive and as we discussed the game standing between the stands and the concession, a lot of the fans walked by with compliments. I guess taking shots builds fan appreciation.

It is seventeen days after surgery; there's no pain and the walker has become something that gets in the way. I got home from my in-patient facility five days ago and quickly discovered that I could sleep better in our La-Z-Boy. The sofa has become something of a nest, the twigs and branches of the nest are my arm rest, pillows, walker, two urinals, two water jugs, exercise instructions, pill bottles, Kleenex, a cell phone, a cordless phone, a sheet, a blanket, a "reacher" (a trigger device that retrieves things - I can't stoop or bend), a keyboard and monitor, a lamp, an end table, and a coffee table. I'm sure it looks like someone has been living here a long time. I'm reminded of pictures of hobos who have carved out spaces amongst earth's garbage for private living quarters.

Dr. Guerra has prescribed sleeping pills, pain killers, anti-inflammatory stuff, and Cumadin, something that thins or thickens my blood depending on the readings of finger pricks twice a week.

Next week starts out-patient therapy in Dr. Guerra's physical therapy facility. I spent three months there after my Harley flip and they like to hurt you.

Five years ago Shelly Derby, the facility's head therapist, was wrenching my broken shoulder and I screamed so loud that she said, "One more like that and I'm throwing you out for the day." She sounded like a damn umpire but she's as good as they get.

Dr. Guerra has told me a couple of times that something about my bone structure made this THR very easy. Apparently the drilling and insertion of the spike into the femur can cause splintering and/or bone punctures. I suppose that all the gluing they do seals everything and eventually everything grows back, strengthening the imperfections.

I have not been without minor setbacks. During late evenings a rash will break out in my armpits, and my palms and insteps itch. The rash reminds me of the hives and the first night it happened, I woke Barb at 2:00am. Things seemed to be erupting all over and I was worried. I've heard of hives clogging up breathing passages. She called Poison Control and they suggested I take some Benadryl and "call my doctor in the morning." The Benadryl took out the rash immediately and I've been off and on it ever since. I'm no longer taking pain medication; it might have been the stuff causing the rash. But I'm pain free and I feel like I could run a mile. But I can't; I'll go from walker to cane and then I'll be healed and playing golf and umpiring.

I would not want another THR tomorrow but considering the trauma, it has not been much of an ordeal. When I have this much free time, I daydream and plan my next attempt at creativity. I'm laying here on the La-Z-Boy, my feet extended, typing and watching a video of the Bee Gees. Barb is on the lanai with Amelia our cat. It's a beautiful day; blue skies and spotty cumulus drifting across my limited view. Barb opens the sliders, pokes her head through and smiling says, "I'll fix our lunch in a few minutes. You should turn off either the video or your monitor because you've *never* been able to multi-task."

But the Bee Gees are singing "Stayin' Alive" and today, at this moment, all of earth is my personal domain and I'm as alive and alert as I've ever been.

Mentally, I *can* multi-task and I can't wait for golf and umpiring and motorcycle riding to start up again, all at once … as long as no one ever asks about me … **"Where did they get this guy?"**